The Self-Esteem Class

The Self-Esteem Class

Simple Lessons for a Lifetime
of Contentment

DR. YOON HONG GYUN

Translated by Jamie Chang

TEN SPEED PRESS
California | New York

TEN SPEED PRESS
An imprint of the Crown Publishing Group
A division of Penguin Random House LLC
1745 Broadway
New York, NY 10019
tenspeed.com
penguinrandomhouse.com

Translation copyright © 2025 by Jamie Chang

Originally published in Korean as *How to Respect Myself* by SimpleLife, South Korea,
in 2016. Copyright © 2016 by Dr. Yoon Hong Gyun. This translation first published
in the United Kingdom by Michael Joseph in 2025. Michael Joseph is part of the
Penguin Random House group of companies.

Typeface: exljbris's Calluna

Library of Congress Cataloging-in-Publication Data is on file with the publisher.

Hardcover ISBN: 978-0-593-83875-4
eBook ISBN: 978-0-593-83876-1

Manufactured in the United States

Editor: Thea Diklich-Newell | Production editor: Serena Wang
Production: Dan Myers
Copyeditor: Nancy Inglis | Proofreaders: Hope Clarke and Tess Rossi
Publicist: David Hawk | Marketer: Monica Stanton

1st Printing

First US Edition

The authorized representative in the EU for product safety and compliance is
Penguin Random House Ireland, Morrison Chambers, 32 Nassau Street,
Dublin D02 YH68, Ireland, https://eu-contact.penguin.ie.

Contents

PART 4

Emotions That Get in the Way of Building Strong Self-Esteem

PART 5

Habits to Break for Self-Esteem Recovery

CONTENTS

PART 6
Things to Overcome for Self-Esteem Recovery

PART 7
Five Practices to Boost Self-Esteem

The Self-Esteem Class

PROLOGUE

Self-Esteem Is the Answer

I am a very happy middle-aged doctor with graying hair. I have my health, my beloved wife and children respect me, my parents trust me, and my brother supports me. On the whole, I have a very good life.

But growing up, I never thought I would turn out so well. I was a frail child. I was sickly and sensitive. I often missed school because of chronic tonsillitis and burst into tears over nothing. I wasn't as outgoing and active as other boys, nor was I clever. I was of average intelligence, and I did not excel at working with my hands, either. I had no confidence or patience. Grown-ups often worried about me.

I was unsure of myself in everything I did. I was a good and obliging kid who always put others first. Looking back, that was my biggest problem. I did not put others first for their sake, but let others take the lead for fear of screwing up. I couldn't trust myself.

Years later, I am not who I thought I'd be. I am very satisfied with my life. I trust my judgment, I love myself, and I am grateful to everyone who helped me become the person I am today.

Some people think that I am happy with my life because

of my status as a psychiatrist, that having a respected job boosted my confidence. They're not entirely wrong. I learned a great deal in my training from good teachers and colleagues. Thanks to them, I was able to grow, and I will always be proud that I am a psychiatrist.

However, I am also aware that there are many unhappy doctors. Psychiatrists have a higher suicide rate compared to other professions. So, if someone were to say that I am happy *because* I have a job that others envy, I would disagree.

A few years ago, I quit my position at a hospital and opened my own practice. One personal goal I set for myself in this period of transition was answering the question "What are the reasons why I am so satisfied with my life?" This was not an easy task. I took the time to write down my thoughts on the meaning of happiness, what makes people happy, and what conditions need to be satisfied. I wanted a record of what I discovered in the process, how it transformed me, and how I could maintain this state of satisfaction.

As the puzzle pieces came together, one concept that kept coming up was *self-esteem,* the dictionary definition of which is "how one perceives oneself," or "indicator of self-love and satisfaction with one's life." I came to focus on this term.

After much reflection, I learned that my road to happiness coincided with my process of building healthy self-esteem. My self-esteem, it turned out, was at its lowest during the most miserable periods in my life.

I was a man of very low self-esteem. I had to repeat a year in medical school, and that wasn't the first time I had failed at something. I did not get into the STEM high school of my choice, nor did I get into the medical program on the first try. Failing my courses in medical school was the biggest blow of them all. I began to question my life goal itself. I drank every day and became addicted to cigarettes and online gaming. The thought of retaking the courses with the first years was demoralizing, and I avoided friends and family out of embarrassment. My med school friends went to school in the morning, and I went to the PC game room. I stayed up all night playing games on the computer and snuck back into the house in the middle of the night. I spent all night in the billiard parlor or went bar-crawling with friends and crept back into the house at dawn.

My self-esteem hit rock bottom on many other occasions besides this, notably during periods when I was lost and in despair. It wouldn't be an exaggeration to say that my life has been a process of rebuilding my flattened self-esteem many times over. Suffering from a deep sense of inferiority and fear that I was falling behind, I was often overcome with the urge to give up and let addiction rob me of all hope for a future.

Looking back, I think the struggle I went through was necessary for restoring my self-esteem, and I can feel true happiness now thanks to my healthy self-esteem. A healthy self-esteem is what led to happiness, and happiness continues to feed my self-esteem. Becoming happy, it turned out, was synonymous with recovering self-esteem. Perhaps this is why the road to building a healthy self-esteem, though difficult and tortuous, was bearable.

Self-esteem turned out to be an important factor in

counseling as well. Most of the unhappy clients who came to me for help needed a self-esteem boost. Some had cheating spouses or were going through breakups; others suffered from depression, addiction, suicidal ideation, and so on. Each needed to work on their self-esteem, and I helped them as their doctor and their self-esteem trainer.

In my training as a psychiatrist, I gained a great deal of knowledge and skills, which I applied to my own life. As a result, I developed a healthier mind and became more empathetic toward others. Based on my own experiences, I learned what not to say to people who are suffering from low self-esteem, how people behave when self-esteem is low, and how to help them. The times I've spent struggling through and overcoming feelings of worthlessness have turned out to be an important asset in my work. I hoped to share the insights I gained in my practice as a doctor and in my personal recovery.

But it wasn't easy to communicate my story and the knowledge I gained through personal experience. Stories from my childhood and my private thoughts, which even my wife does not know about, were hard to divulge. I wrote, deleted, then rewrote the accounts many times. I also had qualms about sharing all my valuable "tricks of the trade." There were some things I did not want other psychiatrists to know. But I decided to write this book anyway for several reasons.

First, I wanted to write this book for myself. I know that my self-esteem is going to weaken again someday. Keeping one's self-esteem healthy is like swimming. Gravity continues to pull us down. I suspect that there will be times in my future when my self-esteem sinks to the bottom, when I make big mistakes or become burned out. I wanted to prepare myself a manual of how to get through those moments when they come.

Second, I decided to write this book for my friends and family. Most of us will experience a crisis of self-esteem at some point in our lives. There were many things I wanted to say to my daughters when they were growing up, but I didn't get around to it either because I didn't have the mountain of information sorted out in my head and I was too busy, or because they were too young to understand. Then I got into a traffic accident last year. It occurred to me that my life could end at any moment and that I could die not having imparted any of my hard-earned wisdom to my children. In a way, this book is a self-esteem guide for my daughters. I think they would much prefer consulting a book to listening to their father give them advice, which probably just sounds like nagging.

Third, I hoped to put into words what I have learned from my career as a psychiatrist. I am ashamed to say that there was a time when I was deeply furious over people plagiarizing the precious information I shared in my writings. As I was starting to enjoy some small fame through my writings, I wondered if it wouldn't be better to keep my hard-earned knowledge to myself. But I soon came to see that knowledge belongs to no one and that I had entertained a very arrogant, dangerous thought in my selfish need for recognition. I now firmly believe that precious information gains greater meaning and potency when shared far and wide.

*

This book is divided into seven main chapters:

- **Part 1** outlines the definition of self-esteem and explains why it is important in our lives. As widely circulated as the word is, *self-esteem* is a term that is frequently misunderstood and misused.
- **Parts 2 and 3** deal with interpersonal relationship problems that arise as a result of low self-esteem.
- **Parts 4 and 5** are on emotions associated with self-esteem.
- **Parts 6 and 7** offer practical approaches to increasing one's self-esteem.

At the end of each chapter, you will find a section entitled "Today's Exercise for Healthy Self-Esteem." Readers will be pleasantly surprised to find that self-esteem can be improved simply by doing the exercises. It will be a useful tool for readers seeking daily regimens for self-esteem improvement.

This book is for anyone who wishes to reflect on their lives, apply the principles of self-esteem to personal challenges, and recover a healthy self-esteem.

Yoon Hong Gyun

PART I

Why Is Self-Esteem Important?

CHAPTER I

The Three Pillars of Self-Esteem

Self-esteem is a fairly common term. Many of us are aware that self-esteem is important. But when asked what self-esteem means, we find that we each have different ideas of it. Some think it is how much one loves oneself, others think it is pride, and still others think it is one's attitude toward oneself. So, before we launch into our discussion, I'd like to provide an exact definition of the term.

The most basic definition of self-esteem is how one evaluates, or "esteems," oneself. In other words, it is a measurement of how highly or poorly one regards oneself. It can be expressed as a numerical value—for instance, 70 out of 100—or verbally as high, average, or low.

The Three Pillars of Self-Esteem

There are three pillars in self-esteem, which incorporate the varied interpretations of self-esteem people have. The three pillars are competence, autonomy, and security.

Competence refers to one's sense of usefulness. This pillar is overemphasized in our society. Competence is why one thinks that having a respected profession or holding an important position at work would raise one's self-esteem.

Autonomy refers to the ability to do as one wishes. Having control over one's life is a vital part of a healthy self-esteem. One might assume that one who attended the best schools and holds degrees from elite institutions would have high self-esteem, but there are plenty among them who have lower self-esteem compared to those who grew up in a country with seemingly unlimited recreational freedom. Lack of autonomy would be the cause of this.

Security is the foundation of self-esteem. Some people have high self-esteem despite having little in life. They excel at feeling secure and comfortable in their surroundings. People with unresolved traumas or a need for affection that cannot be satisfied typically feel unsafe. This of course leads to lowered self-esteem. Equally, those who have trouble being alone may not feel safe alone.

People tend to think that self-esteem refers to how much one loves oneself, and this isn't wrong. Those who regard themselves as worthless, have little control over their own lives, or generally feel unsafe have low self-esteem and consequently have trouble loving themselves, let alone others. Therefore, how much one loves oneself is a good indicator of one's self-esteem.

Confidence, Arrogance, Pride

There are a few concepts that people confuse with self-esteem. I have noticed that a misuse of terms in self-help books has left some of my clients confused. *Confidence, arrogance,* and *pride* are the terms most commonly confused with self-esteem.

Confidence is a concept that measures one's ability relative to the difficulty of a given task. If the ability is strong and the task is perceived as easy, one's confidence rises. On the other hand, if one's level of competence is measured accurately but the task is perceived as too difficult, confidence drops.

Arrogance is the result of overestimating one's ability or underestimating the difficulty of a task. Misreading one's ability leads to overconfidence.

Pride is the emotion associated with self-esteem. If self-esteem is the answer to how one evaluates oneself, pride is the emotion that this evaluation incites. Our pride is said to be hurt when our self-esteem is low. When we are upset because we have been reproached or traumatized, our pride is hurt. "Restoring one's pride" generally means one's pride has recovered from suffering a blow. Thus, *pride* is more often used to depict a negative emotional state.

CHAPTER 2

Misconceptions and Prejudices About Self-Esteem

Misconceptions about self-esteem are just as rampant as confusion about the term itself. Even those who have read volumes on psychology and claim to have a solid foundation misunderstand what it is. Let's look at some of the most common misconceptions about self-esteem.

Self-Esteem Comes from One's Parents

This is a misconception born of information overload. How one is raised and how one is treated as a child are very important, but parents alone do not build their children's self-esteem. People commonly think that lack of affection from parents leads to low self-esteem, but fixation on this notion can have the reverse effect of bringing discord among family members rather than nurturing self-esteem. Belated apologies from parents make little difference; we can rebuild our self-esteem on our own.

Lack of Praise Leads to Low Self-Esteem

"Praise makes even the whales dance" was a common expression in Korea some years ago. This does not mean that praise is always good. Misplaced praise only creates a feeling of emptiness. Delusions about praise can also lead to a sense of inadequacy.

Self-Esteem Is All It Takes to Be Happy

Self-esteem is not an emotion. It is tied to emotion, but strictly speaking, it belongs to the realm of reason. Restoring your self-esteem will not make you feel as though you're floating on air. But higher self-esteem does lead to greater courage. A person with high self-esteem is not overly sensitive to how others see them. They may come home thoroughly exhausted after a long week but do not let it ruin their weekends. They do not let the dread of going to work on Monday mornings ruin their Sunday evenings.

High Self-Esteem Leads to Narcissism

The goal of self-esteem recovery isn't to obtain baseless confidence or to become self-absorbed. Those who have too high an opinion of themselves are called narcissists. They seem arrogant on the surface but live in fear of being shamed. Those with high self-esteem are able to recognize and admit to their shortcomings. They have the strength to accept themselves for the imperfect beings they are and improve themselves.

Can Self-Esteem Truly Be Recovered?

Self-esteem is the measure of how well or poorly one regards oneself. It is a perception and an estimation affected by emotion, which is why it is ever-changing from moment to moment. The changing level of self-esteem may, in turn, cause a wide swing of emotions. Like a roller-coaster ride, the climb is as exhilarating as the drop is terrifying.

The person who has recovered their self-esteem has a decent tolerance for the ups and downs. When their self-esteem is dropping, they are not too afraid, as they know that the seat belt is on and that there is little chance of falling. Same thing on the way up: They prepare for the fall they know will come.

This is one reason why people with healthy self-esteem have good interpersonal relationships. The impact of criticism from others does not linger. A temporary dip in their self-esteem level does not throw them into an emotional slump. Those with healthy self-esteem are regarded as even-keeled.

The long and short of it is that self-esteem can be recovered. It takes time for some, while it is easily accomplished for others. The journey may not be easy, and you may find yourself discouraged. But with effort, self-esteem most certainly can be recovered.

Recovering self-esteem is like learning to ride a bicycle. Much like a bicycle, self-esteem is constantly moving. We get on the saddle of our self-esteem, find our balance, steer, and learn to make the wheels turn.

One usually rides a bicycle alone, but very few people learn to ride a bike all on their own. Even the most athletically gifted person with superb balance needed someone to teach them. They needed someone to coach them and keep them from falling.

Through this book, I hope to explain in detail the structure of this bicycle we call self-esteem and how to ride it safely. I will cover not only how to ride it, but how to ride for a long time without falling, and should you fall, how to do so safely and what protective measures to have in place.

Falling is inevitable when riding a bicycle. Someone can have over thirty years of experience and still fall off occasionally. But the person who knows how to treat the scrape and get back on the bicycle no longer fears it. They will want to ride it often—indeed, begin to rely on it and enjoy it. I wish the same to the readers of this book.

CHAPTER 3

Why Is Self-Esteem Important Today?

What impact does self-esteem have on our lives? In a word, it affects everything—our words, behavior, judgment, choices, and emotions. Self-esteem is especially important today when many people report feeling overwhelmed, because self-esteem is the standard by which one's mental health is measured. Those who consider themselves unhappy, who are having difficulty in their romantic relationships, who have frequent bouts of depression, or who have trouble with interpersonal relationships may be suffering from weakened self-esteem. Social environment is also closely linked to self-esteem. Endless stress and pressure can impact those with even the healthiest self-esteem. In the same vein, those with low self-esteem can gradually recover in a more hospitable social environment.

The Importance of Self-Esteem Today

Why does everything feel so overwhelming for me when other people seem to have no trouble getting married, raising children, and managing their careers?

My clients have been asking this question rather more frequently in recent years. It is never easy to answer this question because I have the same thoughts myself. How is it that other doctors make good money, publish in medical journals, and still make time for their families on weekends, while I still don't own a house, struggle with my research, and find myself exhausted every day? Other people appear to have it easy. They go out and meet people, date, break up, spend a few days under a cloud, then pick themselves right back up again. They have happy marriages and decent jobs.

Could this really be true? Am I feeling unusually alone and overwhelmed while the rest of the world is breezing through life? The short answer is no.

Isolated People in a World Without Barriers

Our lives have improved spectacularly in the past few generations. But the advancement of technology has made it harder to maintain one's mental health. History has proven that there is a strong link between technological advancement and declining mental health. Take, for example, the steep climb in mental health patients in the wake of the Industrial Revolution during the seventeenth century in Britain, many of whom suffered from alcohol addiction.

How has the meteoric development of information technology impacted our lives? Are we happy and healthy in daily lives that begin with checking the news and weather app and staying connected with the world through various platforms until we fall asleep at night?

Smartphones and social media have their advantages. We can connect with people we never would have met at a time when the internet was not available in every home, and in real time, no less. Everyone online is a potential friend, and we become virtual neighbors with people who live on the other side of the planet. Our friends on Facebook, X (formerly Twitter), and blog posts all feature impressive content of beautiful homes, good food, travels abroad, books they've read, and hobbies we admire that leave us feeling bad about ourselves. It depresses us to compare our own lives to the happy lives of others. The admiration fades quickly before a sense of inferiority sets in.

But are they truly as happy and satisfied as they seem? I wouldn't say they are. We may have become more accessible to one another, but that has led to more people putting on an act.

In today's world, the virtual distances between people may have lessened, but the emotional distance has widened. Friendly people can turn out to be foes. We work up the courage to open up, only to be hurt by those we trusted. We are sometimes pilloried because of the comments we make online and find that someone we thought was on our side has turned into a competitor determined to take us down.

Consequently, we do not feel comfortable opening up, and when we do, we constantly censor what we say. We have the option of opening up to anyone we choose, but we don't expect anyone to truly care. This is why most of us, despite being constantly connected, are horribly lonely.

In the past, we went to our siblings with our problems. If a classmate from school took our lunch money, our older siblings could be called upon to get it back for us the next day. When someone insulted us or hurt our feelings, an older sibling comforted us and urged us to stand up for ourselves. But in recent years, siblings cannot be relied upon in the same way, as grown-up siblings are each busy with their own lives. We cannot expect work colleagues or neighbors to offer emotional support, either. We are all islands living with our own troubles. Thus we live in an age where we are connected through many channels yet unable to communicate with one another.

Self-Esteem Is the Most Powerful Resource

It isn't just people that have changed. We live in a world that asks too many questions and makes too many demands. *How are you going to make a living? What do you envision your life to be? Which path will you choose, and when do you plan to reach your goal?* There are so many things we are called upon to decide and justify. It is no wonder that we are confused and anxious. Young people are paralyzed by the question *What am I good at?* They spend all their energy trying to answer this question. We have access to so much more information now, which brings with it more questions and issues that need solutions that are difficult to find. Such is our frustrating reality.

The explosion of information has left us comparing all aspects of our lives against everyone else's, including our very identities. Our thoughts, our life trajectories, our judgments, and the outcomes they yield are compared to those of others. As a result, even those of us who are doing a decent job of managing our lives cannot help but wonder, *Am I really doing okay?*

This social environment has a significant impact on our self-esteem. Constantly comparing ourselves to others, we become increasingly insecure, place the blame on our environments, and even examine our personalities to find problems. The answers to these questions are not easy to find. We feel that something is wrong with us, but with little time to look into the heart of the problem, we stop thinking about it, leaving our self-esteem weakened.

The best defense against challenging circumstances is a healthy mind. The questions of who we are, whether we are on the right path, and if we can handle the road ahead are all matters of self-esteem. A healthy self-esteem helps us navigate our way out of tough times relatively unharmed.

The time has come for each of us to protect our own self-esteem. There is a deluge of writing that offers ideas on how to be happy, but true happiness comes from a robust self-esteem—our greatest weapon for survival in our complicated world.

Self-Esteem Class Summary

- There are three pillars of self-esteem: competence, autonomy, and security.
- Confidence, arrogance, and pride are three concepts often confused with self-esteem.
- Self-esteem is not an emotion. It is affected by emotions but is in the realm of reason. As such, it can be lost, but more important, it can be recovered.
- Loving oneself is a good indicator of one's self-esteem.
- There is a strong link between technological advancement and declining mental health. This is negatively impacting our self-esteem.
- Healthy self-esteem helps us navigate our way out of tough times relatively unharmed.

PART 2

Self-Esteem and Romantic Relationships

CHAPTER 4

Am I Worthy of Love?

Romance is part of all coming-of-age tales. This isn't always because one's sexual desire peaks during adolescence. To grow is to develop a secure self-esteem, which encourages a person to seek out love. In the same vein, one's ability to love and be loved is the first thing that comes into question when one's self-esteem is weakened.

Relationship problems are the issues I encounter most frequently in my work as a psychiatrist. Listening to clients with relationship problems, I inevitably identify a self-esteem problem. Romance is tricky when one's self-esteem is compromised.

Why We Say We Are Not Ready for Relationships

Some people are adamant in their belief that they do not deserve love. Even when they are set up with someone perfectly good-looking and charming, they come up with some flimsy excuse to reject them. When accused of setting their sights too high, they reveal their true thoughts on the matter: *The more someone gets to know me, the more they'll be disappointed.*

Surprisingly, some do not see value in themselves at all. These people may want to be married but at the same time avoid relationships. And if they are in a relationship, they're not sure if their significant other is the right person to marry. They seek out fortune-tellers for answers. They are unsure if they can love someone, if they are even cut out for a relationship that lasts. They label themselves as incapable of relationships and declare that they cannot love and be loved by one person for the rest of their lives. This leads them to the conclusion that they are doomed to live without love. The thought of being alone all their lives leads to a profound sense of loneliness, which makes them crave love all the more.

In spurning the advances of even the most wonderful people, others may find this a shame and urge, "Why give up on such a wonderful person so soon?" They may even say, "You do deserve love." But the belief that one is not lovable is as powerful as a delusion and not easy to shake.

Such people may come across as humble or shy at first, but repetition of self-deprecating behaviors eventually affects interpersonal relationships and generates a great deal of regret. *Maybe I should have worked harder on that relationship,* they might look back and think in their old age.

Weak self-esteem can often lead to a breakup, which then further weakens the self-esteem. The biggest problem of this cycle is that the individual continues to believe after the relationship has broken up that they are undeserving of love. This unfortunately causes them to disparage themselves further and leaves them with less faith in themselves. This is truly a tragedy.

Lack of Basic Trust

Trust is the first step to accepting that we deserve to be loved. This is an essential virtue in our lives. We are all individuals, but we are able to live in societies as teams thanks to our trust in one another. Railway passengers cannot travel if they do not trust their driver. If they start to ask themselves if the driver is properly qualified, they will not have an easy trip.

Trust on such a fundamental level is called *basic trust*. The first basic trust that we establish with another human being is with our mothers. Babies need to trust their primary caregivers to feed them when they're hungry and change them when they've soiled their diapers. If a parent neglects the child or becomes upset when they ask for food, the child fails to establish this first basic trust with the external world. When the parent responds negatively to the child's needs, the child comes to blame themselves for being hungry and regards their very existence as a nuisance.

But a parent's love and parenting style aren't wholly to blame for the absence of basic trust. Basic trust, first formed in the child's relationship with its parents, might later be compromised through various life experiences.

Self-Doubt Ruins Relationships

When we do not have faith in our own charms and competence, we often encounter problems in interpersonal relationships because we begin to question why someone loves us when there is nothing to love. Married people struggling with self-doubt exhibit jealousy or question their partners' faithfulness. When one's self-esteem suffers due to financial difficulties, sexual impotence, or other complexes, one becomes suspicious of others. At the heart of this phenomenon is the idea that *I don't deserve my partner because I'm such a loser.*

When we are in this state, we try to solve the problem by placing the blame on others rather than turning the gaze inward and addressing the sense of inferiority within. It appears as though the pain is coming from loving someone too much, but it is our mistrust of ourselves that plagues us.

A lack of self-worth can even contribute to a person staying in an abusive relationship or allowing themselves to be taken advantage of financially and emotionally. We might stay in bad relationships due to the firm belief that no one else will love us. The relationship goes on because we are afraid of breaking up, not because our love can conquer all.

Give Yourself Attention

These problems arise when we think of ourselves as undeserving of love. But it is worth noting that no one in the world is absolutely, universally deserving of love. No one is perfect in every way, just as no one is completely without worth. There are only people who consider themselves unworthy and undeserving of love.

To find out whether we truly deserve love, we need to take an honest look at ourselves. Did the discord between my parents, for example, have an impact on me? What was the impact? What is my personality? What are my strengths and weaknesses? These are things we must take the time to fully explore.

Better Knowledge Deepens the Affection

Love is an emotion. It cannot be forced. We could repeat the mantra "I am lovable" and still not feel it until we truly love ourselves. No one can snap their fingers and instantly spark self-love. It just does not work that way.

But writing down strengths and weaknesses is a good first step. Coming up with a list of "what others say my strengths are" also works in a pinch. You may think that others' good opinions of you are misguided or the result of knowing you only superficially, but write these down anyway because this process will help you pay close attention to yourself.

All love begins with taking interest. When we love someone, we want to know where they're from or how they spend their days. The small details accumulate over time and become respect and love. Loving ourselves works in the same way. We ought to first get to know who we are and what lives we have lived.

The ability to love another person comes from knowing who you are. The better you know yourself, the better you are able to love.

Today's Exercise for Healthy Self-Esteem: Write About Yourself

Start by taking an interest in yourself. To get to know yourself better, write down your strengths and weaknesses in as much detail as possible.

1. What are my strengths and weaknesses?
2. What am I good at? What am I not good at?
3. What do others say I'm good at?

CHAPTER 5

People Who Question
Their Worth

When we do not love ourselves, we feel awful, as if we are stuck with a bully who picks on us all day. We feel criticized and pessimistic when we've done nothing wrong. But when we love ourselves, life becomes simpler. We feel we are with a good friend when we spend time alone. Loneliness does not escalate to anguish, and we can turn to ourselves for guidance when we are lost. This does not mean that we become loners when we love ourselves, but that we do not fear being alone. This gives us confidence, which dispels the anxiety we feel when we are with others and comes off as a positive personality trait that makes us well liked in our communities.

I Don't Like Myself

There was a time when I couldn't stand myself. Toward the end of my first year of high school, I went through a period of lethargy. I couldn't get myself out of bed in the morning or work up an appetite, and I lost interest in everything. I stopped bathing, and when I did make it to school, I sat in the back of the classroom staring off into space or napping.

A lifelong model student up to that point, I could hardly recognize myself. But I had too little energy left in me to be shocked into taking action. Classmates whispered among themselves that I was sleeping through classes because I was up all night studying, but I couldn't even be bothered to set them straight.

I didn't lash out at anyone, nor did I express my frustrations. My family did not seem to notice, either. My older brother thought I was irritable because of the upcoming college entrance exams. I questioned my family's interest in me and came to believe that they never cared about me in the first place.

One day my mother asked me to come on a walk with her. She took me to a local bookstore and said, "Get all the books you want." I browsed the shelves and picked a book called *How to Love Myself.* The tag line *I cannot love anyone if I don't love myself* caught my eye. From that day on, any time I couldn't find the will to do anything, I flipped through this book.

Looking back, there was one thing that frustrated me more during this period than suffering from lethargy— I didn't know what was happening to me. I hated myself for being so weak, unmotivated, and defeatist, and I couldn't understand why I was feeling this way. It was awful to be seized with self-hatred. It might have been less painful if I could pinpoint the exact cause that had led to my helpless state, like poor grades or troubles at home.

I don't remember the specifics of *How to Love Myself*, but I do know that it played an important role in teaching my seventeen-year-old self why I needed to love myself and what would happen if I didn't. What I learned from this book gave me the courage to navigate my way out of difficult times in the years to come. I used the question "How can I love myself under these circumstances?" as my compass. No matter how important a person was to me, I did not prioritize the relationship at the expense of my self-esteem. I was able to get a clean break from people who hurt me and made me miserable. I applied the same approach when battling addictions to alcohol and online gaming. My life was more important to me than socializing with drinkers or collecting rare game items.

Years later, I am a psychiatrist who tends to my clients' minds. People who cannot love themselves come to me for help, and I find myself particularly compelled to help them. This is probably because I know all too well how awful it is to be in their shoes.

When I suffered another period of lethargy in my twenties, I could not figure out the cause of it then, either. I was not as industrious as I wanted to be, and I did not like that about myself. I suspect the reason for this was that I was raised by very hardworking parents, and on top of that, I was addicted to overburdening myself with work.

The feeling of self-hate continued through college. Medical school was full of people who were smarter and more hardworking than me, who could even outdrink me. I kept telling myself that I was awkward and slow to learn compared to my classmates. The sense of inferiority grew.

But I was too embarrassed to talk about it with anyone. Friends who chose other paths were in college or studying for civil service exams, envious of my college life. I figured they would think I was complaining over nothing. But more important, I didn't know how to seek empathy when I didn't understand what I was feeling myself. I got through this period without sharing these thoughts with anyone. Looking back, that was when I learned that self-hate can leave a person feeling very lonely.

I Am My Best Friend

All of us have people we like or dislike. It is not problematic to dislike or be indifferent toward another person. But disliking someone close to us does create problems. We cannot expect to be happy if we are indifferent toward our significant others or do not love our spouses. Having someone in our family or at work whom we dislike can also create stress. A marriage without love negatively impacts the children. Therefore, it goes without saying that we are miserable when we dislike ourselves.

When we dislike ourselves, we are confronted with a person we dislike every moment of every day, even when we are doing mundane tasks like speaking, eating, or sleeping. Each time we look in the mirror, we see someone we don't like.

When we do not love ourselves, we are constantly irritable, whether we are aware of it or not. We compare ourselves to others and disparage ourselves for being too helpless, too short, too sensitive. Picture someone hanging on your back all day whispering in your ear, "You're a loser. You can't do anything right." That is what it means to hate yourself. While we have the option of distancing ourselves from those who attack us, we are stuck with the critical voice when we hate ourselves. The constant comparisons and criticisms build up over time and lower our self-esteem, making us more disparaging toward ourselves.

When we love ourselves, however, many aspects of life are easier. Loving oneself is like being with a good friend. Those who love themselves do not have a difficult time with loneliness and even enjoy traveling alone. They are comforted each time they look at themselves in the mirror and find their own voices reassuring. They can soothe and encourage themselves. They do not replay their actions in their heads and worry about how their behavior could have been misinterpreted by others.

Of course, we experience distress even when we love ourselves. We might fail an exam, break up with a significant other, or lose a parent. But hardship does not lead to self-disparagement when we love ourselves, as we are able to accept tough realities for what they are and let the pain pass.

When we love ourselves, we are able to actively look for solutions. We do not waste energy criticizing and blaming ourselves. Just as a healthy immune system helps us recover faster from infections, we leave ourselves less vulnerable when protected with self-love. It's like having a caring, encouraging friend with us at all times.

Tell Yourself That It's Okay

Tell yourself often that you're okay. Too long have we measured ourselves against others and found ourselves inferior and reprehensible. We have needlessly condemned ourselves as abnormal and inadequate. We have been living in sorrow for a long time due to unfair criticism. So, starting now, we ought to comfort ourselves often, to the point where it feels excessive. One might worry that too much encouragement might make one self-complacent, but that is unlikely to happen. It is especially important to actively build yourself up if you've been denying yourself or putting yourself down. Tell yourself that it isn't your fault. That society and education are to blame. Feel free to project. Be overly generous to yourself and make excuses for yourself. Tell yourself that it's okay to become self-complacent.

It's okay. It's okay if your self-esteem is low. The period of lethargy will allow you to recharge, and the recovery will encourage you to grow. For now, tell yourself that you're doing okay and you're doing enough. It's okay if you can't bring yourself to say it right away. We've just taken our first step.

Today's Exercise for Healthy Self-Esteem: "It's Okay" Journal

Take the time to look back on your day and encourage yourself. This exercise will teach you to be more sympathetic to yourself and to those you love as well.

1. What happened today?
   For example, *I read a book about self-esteem.*

2. What feelings come up when you look back on the event?
   For example, *I am worried that I might have low self-esteem.*

3. Tell yourself, *It's okay.*
   For example, *It's okay to be worried that a book about self-esteem is making me question my self-esteem. It's a normal way to feel after reading such a book. It would be strange if I didn't. I'm okay.*

CHAPTER 6

Love That Demands
Constant Validation

One might assume that popular or well-loved people have high self-esteem. But many celebrities these days suffer from depression. Despite ample evidence of popular acclaim and attention, some celebrities feel anxious, lonely, and unworthy of love. The more they try to make up for their inadequacies by embellishing and putting on a front, the more wretched they feel inside.

When confidence runs low, we start to wonder if there is a soul in the world who could love us for who we are. Convinced that a decent person could never love us, we become enamored with someone who is clearly not good for us.

With Love Comes Obsession

When self-esteem is running low, we do not take confessions of love from decent people seriously. We are skeptical at first, then clingy in the end. Some believe that this is the result of loving too deeply, but this is obsession. Obsession is an illness, and like most illnesses, it wears down and drives away even the most devoted partners.

When a relationship breaks up because of obsessive behavior, our self-esteem plummets even further. *See? Another one left me. Of course they didn't love me,* we say to ourselves. We obsess because of low self-esteem, which in turn lowers the self-esteem even more. This is an unfortunate vicious cycle.

In the book *Non-Possession,* by the Zen Master Monk Beopjeong, he writes about tending to his orchid plant. The monk finds great delight in looking after a potted orchid plant he receives as a present. It brings him great joy to water it, give it sunlight, and admire it. But before long, he realizes that his love for the plant brings with it worries in equal amounts: *What if it withers or freezes while I'm away for several days?*

Anyone who has kept a living thing, like a dog or a plant, will identify with the monk's story. When we feel affection toward something, it brings us fear as well as delight. When the object of our affection is another person, we call it love. Two people in love, while in raptures over each other, also feel fearful that the relationship might end. A new couple spends the first three months of a relationship quarreling and making up. They argue, resolve their differences, restore affection for each other, then argue some more. Through this process, the relationship becomes stable.

But acclimatizing to a new relationship presents those of us with low self-esteem with a period of emotional upheavals. It's difficult to find love when we have low self-esteem, but when we do, we get into arguments much sooner in the relationship, blow conflicts out of proportion, and struggle to reconcile. In this process, our self-esteem suffers even more as we are chagrined by the insecure, obsessive side that love brings out in us.

You Said You Loved Me—How Could You?

We fall in love for many reasons. Because we meet someone who's kind, well-read, good-looking, or guileless or even because we feel bad for them or can't stop thinking about them. Sometimes we fall in love for no conceivable reason at all.

There are times when we love someone for the sole reason that they loved us first. This of course is about us, not about the person we love. We think, *It's very special that you love me when no one else does.* We come to think that the person who loves us is *the only person who could ever love us.* When we love someone for their looks or for their money, we love them for qualities that they have. But when we love someone because they love us, the underlying thought is that this person is special not because of any quality that belongs to them, but because they love us when we do not deserve love.

When our self-esteem is healthy, we operate on the belief that we are lovable and that it is natural for someone to love us. This belief is an important foundation for nurturing love. But when we don't see our charms or value ourselves, love becomes a challenge.

Arguments break out in relationships when we question

the belief that our partner loves us. We think that we are fighting because our partner forgot an anniversary, canceled a date, or does not call often, but the underlying problem is often that we think they no longer love us. We think something along the lines of *If you love me, how can you go for so long without calling? If you love me, how can you be so affectionate toward another person? If you love me, how can you not remember our special day?* The rhetorical questions that start the arguments contain the need for confirmation that our partner loves us. A response to this might be *I do love you. But I can't call when I'm busy. If you really loved me, you would be more understanding.* A few more of these back-and-forths turn an argument into an all-out fight. A little spat is not a problem, but when a couple fights over the same issue many times and fundamentally doubts that they love each other, the cause is typically low self-esteem.

When we do not believe that we deserve love, we are suspicious of the people who love us. Love, even when the object is a potted orchid or a dog, requires a great deal of energy and effort. So it is no wonder that relationships cannot last when one person is always asking skeptically, "Do you even love me?"

People with low self-esteem sometimes speak in layers of codes. For example, "What took you so long?" does not simply communicate, *I'm upset that you're late,* but also, *You think so little of me that you don't bother showing up on time.* And underneath this message is the suspicion, *Now that you've got to know me better, you don't love me anymore.*

With so much at stake, the spat quickly turns into an intense argument as the couple find themselves with so much more to address than simply being tardy. Just for being late to dinner, one partner must apologize, must offer assurance to the other that they love them and that the other will continue to be deserving of love. The fight itself is so draining that the couple has no energy left to discuss methods of being on time.

When people with low self-esteem get into relationships, they become preoccupied with the flaws in their own personalities and their appearances. Their traumas, need for validation, and other inadequacies take attention away from their partners. Lack of self-esteem, not of love, is clearly the issue.

Lovers' Spats

Relationships look different for people with healthy self-esteem. Those of us who believe that we deserve love do not make mountains out of emotional molehills. We may become upset and worried when our partners do not show up to a date on time, but it does not lead to our questioning our self-worth. When we argue, we take issue with our partner's being late and nothing more. We are upset because our partner kept their phone off for several hours while out drinking well past midnight, or because they were very late to a date twice in a row. Then we go straight to coming up with a solution together.

Those of us with healthy self-esteem do get upset or resentful from time to time as well. We do get angry when we feel that we are not being treated with the love and respect we deserve. But the fights do not turn vicious. We do not wound each other by letting an argument become too emotional. Instead, we address the hurt feelings and come up with plans for modifying behavior. We are good at communicating what our partner needs to do to keep us from worrying in the future when they're late. We are able to keep our focus on encouraging change in our partner while meeting them halfway ourselves.

Love brings much happiness but requires a great deal of energy in return. When we do not waste energy on questioning whether our partner really loves us or whether we are truly lovable, we can focus all our energy on building a healthy relationship.

A Strong Foundation for Love

Seeing yourself for the lovable person that you are is an essential foundation in nurturing a loving relationship. A stable relationship is impossible without it. One important reason why relationships fail despite all our efforts is because we keep forgetting that we deserve love.

Many of us love and strive to be loved. We try to look nice, alter the way we speak and act, and even change jobs and careers for it. But self-love is the crucial element that will allow us to focus on our relationship with the one we love. When we are insecure about our worth, our energy is often misplaced; we focus on ourselves when we ought to be paying attention to our partner, and doubt the partner when it is ourselves we cannot trust.

If this is your relationship pattern, try shifting your perspective. For example, when choosing outfits or getting a new haircut, prioritize looking good *for yourself,* not for others. To anyone who worries that this line of thinking would make a person self-absorbed, I would say that it's okay. We care too much about what others think of us and whether we are worthy in their eyes. We need to shift that focus onto ourselves, be kinder to ourselves, and take interest in what we want.

Today's Exercise for Healthy Self-Esteem: Treat Yourself

A gift is a gesture of affection. When we love someone, we want to buy gifts for them. We treasure gifts from significant others and remind ourselves of how much they love us. A gift can have a powerful effect.

So give yourself a gift. Ask yourself what gift would be good for you and what you would be most happy to receive. And when you've picked a present for yourself, pat yourself on the back, *Great choice! I'm really good at choosing gifts!* This will take you one step closer to loving yourself. Some people may find treating themselves disingenuous or overdone. Others may wonder, *What have I done to deserve nice things? Or How will this help me love myself?* If you find yourself unwilling to embrace the idea of treating yourself, this is further proof that you have been neglectful of yourself. It's all the more reason to be good to yourself. Just get yourself something you know you will enjoy.

CHAPTER 7

Warring Couples
Who Cannot Break Up

A couple may fight every now and then, but frequent fights are a red flag, and justifying the frequent fights as a sign of passion is a dangerous line of thinking. Even couples with high self-esteem fight sometimes. But their fights do not escalate, and they make up quickly. They do not fight to wound each other's pride. They know when to stop.

One Year Later, If You're Still Fighting

Most marriage problems come from dissimilar communication styles. Raised by different parents and under different circumstances, two people are bound to communicate in different ways. There are bound to be conflicts in the adjustment period as two people learn to talk to each other, and through this process, their bond is strengthened.

Most couples fight less frequently and enter a period of stability within three to six months from the start of the relationship. If the couple fails to reach a compromise, they break up. But if one person has significantly lower self-esteem than the other, the relationship becomes stuck in limbo. The couple continues to attack and assign blame, unable to love each other or part ways.

If you've been in a relationship for over a year and the fighting has not stopped, check your self-esteem. Some couples pride themselves on their ability to make up quickly after their frequent fights, but the way the fight is resolved matters. Even if we manage to resolve an intense argument and walk away from it without lingering resentments, we cannot erase its impact on the brain and skin.

If you win a fight, what then? You've just subdued the person you love. When you "defeat" your partner, you may relish your victory in the short term, but at what cost? The subdued partner is overcome with profound dejection that comes from being attacked by the one who is supposed to love them.

A couple is a team, and the emphasis should be on finding common ground and understanding. Even the strongest teams have their disagreements, but sabotaging your own team is a foolish course of action.

The Real Reason Why We Fight

People who cannot trust themselves do not have faith in the relationships they form with others. First of all, they cannot be sure if it was the right decision to enter into a relationship to begin with. So they keep asking themselves,

Is this the right time for me to be dating? Is this the right person for me? Won't they leave me, too?

Being attracted to or developing a crush on someone falls in the realm of instinct. But dating is different. Dating is a decision, not an inclination. A crush is a feeling, but a relationship is a conscious choice. So if you cannot trust your judgment, the relationship will create anxiety.

The same goes for those of us who do not love ourselves. No matter how loved we are, we do not understand why the one we're with loves us. We wonder, *Why would someone as great as you want to be with me? Are you just into my looks?* We become suspicious, and our skeptical view of the relationship soon becomes obvious.

When we undervalue ourselves, we inversely demand too much from a relationship. Rather than being happy in an ordinary romantic relationship, we expect profound connection on a fundamental metaphysical level. We overcompensate for the love we did not receive as children or expect a powerful love story instead of simply dating.

When we are in this state, we cannot make stable emotional connections. We are anxious on dates and doubtful when our significant other says, "I love you." We grow more obsessive and more nervous as we fall deeper in love. We waste energy trying to calm our fears. What ensues is an environment ripe for conflict.

Inflicting Deep Wounds

The difference between a fight and a conversation is that the former aims to attack. When lovers fight, there is more at stake than when strangers do. Two people who are close and know a lot about each other can inflict lasting wounds on each other. A fight with your lover can obliterate your last remaining scrap of self-esteem.

This is why fights between lovers and spouses can be so harmful. The closer two people are, the better they know each other's weaknesses and which buttons to press. Intimate knowledge of each other becomes weaponized and comes out as *That's always been your problem. That's why you get no respect at work,* or *You're just like your mother.* The fight does not have to be physical for couples to end up wounded and devastated at the end of it.

It is painful to discover that one cannot love in a healthy way. We start to keep things from our significant other. Love, which is supposed to feed our self-esteem, brings on self-disparagement.

Love Should Not Hurt So Much

We all have fantasies of love, that love will make us happy. This belief is prevalent in both Eastern and Western cultures, from Chunhyang to Cinderella. We think that true love will cure all pain.

The same goes for self-esteem. Many people think that

love will nurture self-esteem. People with painful pasts hope to heal themselves through love and attain happiness. Just as a romantic relationship is the first thing we gravitate toward when self-esteem is restored, we also seek out love when self-esteem runs low.

That is why people with low self-esteem have a difficult time ending relationships. They suffer through relationships they don't want. They become emotionally depleted and depressed but still cannot work up the courage to break up. Surviving on the occasional *I love you* or hints of affection based on no real evidence, they keep the hopeless relationship alive. As the emotional upheavals continue to wear a person down, they protect the relationship with their lives under the belief that no one else in the world will love them or that they will never survive the breakup. They sink into despair, as they believe that staying in this relationship, no matter how destructive, is their only hope. The relationship becomes a source of sadness.

One surprising thing I found as a psychiatrist is how many patients confuse sadness with love. They think they're experiencing the pain of love when they're crying out of anger, depressed because of fear, and heartbroken from sadness. Pain is just pain. To quote the Everly Brothers, "Love hurts." But love that hurts too much isn't love. Sometimes breaking up is the fastest path to happiness.

Today's Exercise for Healthy Self-Esteem: The Loving Prayer

You don't have to love the person you're with for the rest of your life. It might even be a good idea to break up sooner rather than later. This is not a call to sabotage your relationship when you're in love. Don't worry about the possibility of the relationship ending in the future. Don't test or torment the person you love and pray that your love deepens as a result.

Love is a complicated feeling that often creates confusion. Some confuse distrust and bossiness with love. But the important thing is to love with abandon while you are in love. So say a prayer before bed every night: "Let my love for this person grow."

CHAPTER 8

Overcoming Fear of Breaking Up

The Fear of Breakups

Some people are uncommonly afraid of breakups. Even when they no longer wish to continue a relationship, the fear of ending it prevents them from walking away. Friends and family might advise them to move on, and they themselves might realize that the relationship is unsalvageable, yet they cannot bring themselves to part ways. They endure the unhappiness, sometimes even staying with a partner who neglects or abuses them. They might lend significant amounts of money without asking for repayment because they fear asserting their rights might drive their partner away.

The Breakup Clinic

The Breakup Clinic is a section in my online blog. Many people who are experiencing overwhelming fear at the prospect of a breakup or are struggling to recover from a breakup visit my counseling practice after reading entries from this section, but the challenge of breaking ties does not apply to romantic relationships alone.

People who seek help at the Breakup Clinic generally fall into two categories. The first excessively idealizes their former partner. They often claim that their exes were the perfect match for them. They place their ex on a pedestal, unable to think rationally due to the sadness and shock of the breakup. The second group becomes addicted to self-pity and grief. They drown in the sorrow and misery of the breakup. Falling into self-pity is similar to being intoxicated. Once you begin to feel sorry for yourself, it is easy to get carried away. It is no surprise that those who frequently indulge in self-pity are at a higher risk of developing alcohol addiction. Seeing themselves as pitiful, they come to crave sympathy from themselves and others.

People who fear breakups often stigmatize breakups as entirely negative. They act as if life itself will end with the breakup, succumbing to despair before taking the time to truly notice which aspect of the breakup hurts the most. They fear loneliness. They equate being alone with being miserable and believe they can never be happy alone. Thinking of themselves as too weak and helpless to do anything on their own, they cannot end relationships that no longer work. They undervalue themselves, telling themselves, *I need that person. They are the only one who loves me,* or *No one has ever loved me like they do.*

Distressing Memories of Being Left Alone

Fear of breakups is often linked to past wounds, particularly the trauma of being left alone. Many such negative associations are formed when children are left alone or feel abandoned by their parents. If something scary or unpleasant happened while they were on their own, they can grow very fearful of being alone. This fear often extends to resentment toward parents, who are blamed for abandoning their child. The memories of being neglected and without protection leave a person fearful of finding themselves in that vulnerable position again.

If a child is praised for their bravery after being scared and alone, the experience may not leave lasting negative effects, as it is an opportunity for the child to overcome anxiety and build courage. However, if the child experiences major incidents while alone, such as sexual abuse, it can leave a lasting wound. Even without major incidents, a lack of sufficient empathy for the child's anxiety at being alone can also leave scars. Childhood bullying and isolation can also leave a person fearful of being deserted.

Breaking Up Is Hard for Everyone

Breakups are not easy. If losing a long-cherished object can make you feel anxious and empty, it is no surprise that parting from a person can be painful. It's important to remember that everyone finds breakups challenging. If you are struggling with a breakup, know that this is a common human experience. We each deal with it in our own way. Some might accept it as fate, as I do, though it took time for me to reach that point. Everyone has a different way of coping that can evolve over time.

Be gentle with yourself regarding how you react to a breakup. Some cry for days, some laugh as if nothing happened, some get angry, and some feel numb. There are no rules on how to react or rules against being angry or keeping your feelings bottled up.

Breaking Up as an Opportunity for Self-Care

There's no need to label a breakup as something entirely bad. Just as there are no purely good events, there are no purely bad ones. Being alone after a breakup might make you feel lonely, but it also brings freedom. I realized this while treating mothers in their thirties struggling with depression. Their common desire was to "experience being alone." From the moment a woman becomes pregnant, she loses her freedom, as she is constantly called upon to make the child's health her first priority. She loses autonomy on what to eat and drink and what activities to engage in. And when the child is born, the mother can hardly find time for her most basic biological needs like feeding herself, sleeping, or simply going to the bathroom.

Working moms and stay-at-home moms alike rarely have time to rest or get a good night's sleep. They may feel the loss of the freedom they used to have. They need space and miss the feeling of loneliness. "I just want to go for a run in an empty park," a client once said tearfully.

Conversely, many women in their fifties and sixties are heartbroken over the idea of being left alone. After twenty years of anticipating the day their children would leave the nest, some mothers struggle with feelings of emptiness when this period in their lives finally arrives. On the other hand, some women enjoy their newfound freedom, recognizing it as an opportunity to live without catering to their family's needs.

When you find yourself alone, think of it as a precious opportunity to do whatever you please with your time and resources. While being with a loved one brings joy, it also comes with its share of constraints. You need to consider and respect your partner's feelings just as much as you receive their care and respect. When you are alone, you get to focus on yourself without needing anyone's approval or putting up with nagging and unsolicited advice.

When a client is struggling after a breakup, I often recommend that they take a trip. Traveling solo might seem a bit lonely at first, but most find it incredibly satisfying once they set off. You can choose your own travel dates and preferred means of transport, and plan your itinerary without having to coordinate with anyone else. Even if the destination turns out to be less than ideal, it doesn't matter. Once you experience this freedom, you'll find yourself appreciating the value of solitude, and even come to see that being alone isn't so bad after all.

After parting ways with a loved one, it's important to take time to reflect on what you gained and learned from the relationship. You don't need to plan an elaborate trip; a day trip or revisiting familiar places can be just as fulfilling. I personally wandered around familiar spots in Seoul. I got on the underground and pretended I was a foreigner who had just arrived. This mindset made the experience enjoyable. If it wasn't for my newfound freedom, I would not have attempted it.

Today's Exercise for Healthy Self-Esteem: Say Goodbye to Bad Habits

Breakups provide an excellent opportunity to develop your resilience to loneliness. No matter how happy you are now, you will inevitably face a painful separation someday. Practicing for this can help mitigate the psychological impact when it happens. (Of course, this doesn't mean you should end your healthy relationship with your partner or family members.) For this exercise, practice breaking away from bad habits. It's time to give up habits like sleeping in late, binge-eating at night, or drinking and smoking excessively. Bad habits often lead to addiction and enslave us. Breaking free from them grants us freedom.

Make a list of the habits you wish to break and note the benefits of letting them go.

Examples:

I want to break the habit of binge-eating at night. This will improve my health.

I want to stop being critical of myself. This will help me feel more confident.

I want to quit the habit of constantly changing lanes to pass other cars. This will reduce the risk of accidents.

I want to reduce screen time. This will decrease fatigue and provide more leisure time.

I want to avoid bottling up emotions only to blow up later. This will prevent feelings of regret and self-blame.

I want to stop calling my ex late at night. This will spare me shame and embarrassment.

CHAPTER 9

Putting on a Mask for Fear of Being Disliked

Some people are exceptionally cheerful and friendly. These people turn heads the moment they enter a room. They act as if they've found a lifelong friend in you, displaying a level of intimacy and even flirting as if they are enchanted by you. You might feel as if you've formed an instant, close bond with them. However, upon reflection, you may realize you know almost nothing about them. These individuals tend to show only their best sides, seldom forming a genuine connection with others. True relationships involve accepting each other's flaws, not just a pretty facade.

Wanting Love vs. Fearing the Loss of Love

Many people desire to be loved. While living independently can bring happiness, humans are inherently social beings. Being respected and appreciated by others is a fundamental requirement for self-esteem. The easiest way to perceive oneself as a lovable person is to receive love from others.

The desire to be loved is not inherently problematic. The issue arises when we place excessive importance on being loved. This natural desire can easily turn into an obsession. The fear of not being loved can be just as strong as the desire to be loved. This anxiety is a central theme in Ichiro Kishimi's bestseller, *The Courage to Be Disliked*, which reflects a common fear.

Just as an intense desire to pass an exam can increase the fear of failing, the pressure to win a game can impair performance. Parents who excessively wish for their child to be loved by everyone might say things like "You'll be ostracized if you do that," or "What will people think?" When parents value social approval, they can instill the belief in their child that the consequences of not being loved are catastrophic. This obsession with other people's approval becomes a fear of being disliked.

Pursuing Happiness vs. Avoiding Misery

People who focus on what they want often visualize achieving their goals. Students who want to excel in school imagine themselves succeeding and try to emulate the behaviors that lead to good grades. Even when they fall short, they tend to analyze what went wrong and make efforts to produce better results the next time around.

In contrast, those who aim to avoid what they do not want complicate things for themselves. When the goal is to avoid poor academic performance, for example, the underlying motivation is often the belief that a student who performs poorly is unworthy. This differs from those who believe that good grades bring recognition. When a student's goal is to avoid bad performance, any drop in grades can be devastating, as it means they have become what they do not want to be. They associate their worth with their grades, leading to a negative self-image that comes from equating "student who gets bad grades" with "unworthy person" with "me."

When we focus on excelling in school, we naturally pay more attention to the strategies of successful students and learn how they overcome challenges. Conversely, focusing on avoiding failure leads to understanding the traits and experiences of cautionary tales. Careful research into how the failures are treated externally and how crushing the blow can be causes us to develop a fear of those outcomes.

If we always get the grades we want or expect, pursuing what we want and avoiding what we don't want may yield similar outcomes. But most lives include ups and downs and periods of difficulty. The difference between aiming for happiness and avoiding misery becomes evident when we come upon roadblocks.

Negative Goals Breed Fear

What happens when someone doesn't aim to be loved but rather fears being unloved? Fear of rejection leads the brain to conjure scenarios of being unloved: being overlooked by teachers, ostracized by peers, gossiped about at school or work, and feeling lonely. To avoid these scenarios, one strives to be liked, always smiling and trying to look and act charming.

Unfortunately, we cannot avoid setbacks. Even the most lovable person on earth cannot be adored by all. It happens to the best of us—never hearing back from the person we had a lovely date with or being dumped by our partner.

In such situations, people with negative goals tend to dwell on their shortcomings, asking themselves what makes them unlovable. They focus on their perceived flaws and go over every word and gesture that could have been seen in a negative light, such as when they were angry at someone or when they were too greedy. Thoughts like *People will be disappointed in me* or *They'll be dismissive of me* begin to crop up. And the unfailingly problematic perception that one is uniquely flawed—*I'm too different!*—adds fuel to the fire, leading the individual to believe that their unique flaws make them especially unlovable. Fear thus piles up and threatens to cause an emotional explosion.

Fear Is Not a Vaccine

This mindset isn't rational. Friends and family might say, "Why would anyone be disappointed in you? You're so lovely and capable." If the person can see that their friends and family are right, that would be ideal. If they can overcome the fear, they can simply say, "You're right. I must be stressed from work. I'm not weird, am I?"

However, when engulfed in fear, rational discussion becomes impossible. Logic cannot get through the emotional walls we put up. Fear of rejection and isolation can be so overwhelming that it blocks communication. Conversation, a logical exchange of ideas between two people, cannot progress when one is stuck at *I'm afraid people will be disappointed in me. I just am.* This is because fear of not being loved is amplified by past experiences of rejection. Even minor criticisms from a boss can trigger profound dejection and anxiety; one small comment from your boss leaves you tearful and convinced that no one in the world likes you. The fear can also bring up a sense of injustice and anger.

People with deep-seated fears often interpret criticism as an attack on their character, not just their work. They think, *Why do they hate me so much?* Those already dissatisfied with themselves are worse off in these situations. They might think, *I am really bad at this. It's no wonder my boss called me out.* They believe they've been exposed for the fraud that they are, leading to self-stigmatization.

Low self-esteem not only damages relationships but is also a result of troubled relationships. Experiencing conflict and feeling hurt lead to self-deprecating thoughts like *I'm not professional*, or *I'm so sensitive I hang on to little criticisms forever.*

Sadly, the source of debilitating, irrational fears can be traced back to childhood. In disciplining their children, parents might say, "People won't like you if you act that way." They believe that fear of being rejected will make the child strive to be likable, but it does not work that way. Fear is not a vaccine against bad behavior. It depletes self-esteem, which works as an antibody when we are attacked by the virus called rejection. Fear and anxiety take over in the absence of self-esteem, depriving us of the chance to assess the situation with emotional clarity.

Confidence Is Appealing

No one is universally likable. We are bound to face rejections, and we are bound to disappoint. Our hearts cannot be filled with beauty alone. Everyone has issues within. We have greed, jealousy, and perhaps some desires that would shock others. We may lack confidence and need to lean on others for support. We simply keep these things hidden. All these elements combined are referred to as the id. Everyone has an ego and a benevolent self that controls it, called the superego. While beauty and charm represent the superego, the id is the side of us that we'd rather hide. Everyone, whether they are loved or love others, has an id. Therefore, there is no need to feel ashamed of having an id.

If you are not loved, it is not your fault. Just as failing an exam does not make you a bad student.

Today's Exercise for Healthy Self-Esteem: Apologize to Yourself

This evening, stand in front of a mirror and apologize to yourself. Say aloud, "I'm sorry for hating myself over such trivial things. I'm so sorry for not being confident and hiding my true feelings."

We have been less than kind to ourselves. We fail to accept ourselves as we are. We disliked our appearance, our personality, and our situation in life. We are ashamed of our reality and our unspoken dreams.

We deserve better, and it begins with an apology to ourselves. This marks the difference between our past selves with low self-esteem and our new selves striving to change.

When apologizing to yourself, avoid making unnecessary excuses. Don't say, "I pushed myself hard because I wanted to succeed," or "If I were a more competent person, I wouldn't be so afraid of failure." Simply acknowledge the ways you have hurt yourself and sincerely apologize for them.

PART 2 CONCLUSION

It's Neither Love's Fault
nor Yours

If you have self-esteem issues, you likely struggle with love. You'll feel suspicious whether you want to or not, spend more time arguing than enjoying being together, frequently become upset at your partner's indifference, or feel lonely thinking you love your partner more than they love you. You might even despise these feelings and spiral into self-reproach.

But you don't have to wait until your self-esteem is fully restored before you can love. Society has fantasies about love because love is indeed a powerful thing. It can both chip away at your self-esteem and heal it.

If you're in a troubled relationship but can't let go, there's likely a reason. It might be better to argue with the hope of working things out than to separate entirely when there is lingering affection in the relationship. When in doubt, don't rush to end things or beat yourself up for not being decisive.

Your struggles may stem from various sources beyond self-esteem. You might be exhausted or stressed from money problems. Don't jump to the conclusion that love is the only problem, or that love is inherently painful and not for you. It is enough to acknowledge that your self-esteem issues can make emotional intimacy a challenge. We have much more to discuss, and the real journey begins now.

Self-Esteem Class Summary

- One's ability to love and be loved is the first thing that comes into question when one's self-esteem is weakened.
- Trust is an essential virtue and the first step needed in accepting that we deserve love.
- When self-doubt creeps in, it is important to address the sense of inferiority within.
- The better you know yourself, the better you are able to love.
- Take the time to be your own cheerleader. Work on being generous and encourage yourself. The work you do within will radiate out.
- Rifts in relationships can almost always be attributed to low self-esteem.
- Sometimes it is easy to confuse sadness with love. The truth is, pain is just pain. If you find yourself crying out of anger or depressed because of fear, breaking up may be the fastest path to happiness.

- Aiming for happiness and avoiding misery are not guaranteed means of achieving success or happiness.
- Fear is often irrational; do not let it govern or cloud your emotional clarity.

PART 3

Self-Esteem and Social Relationships

CHAPTER 10

How Much Recognition
Do I Receive?

Self-esteem, in its most common sense, means self-respect. It refers to how much you respect yourself and perceive yourself as a valuable person. The understanding of the importance of self-esteem is growing, and this is evident in modern parenting books, which emphasize the importance of praising and clearly expressing love for children. Thanks to more awareness and conscientious parents, today's children likely have higher self-esteem compared to older generations.

Unfortunately, many of today's adults did not grow up hearing affirmations like "You are a valuable person." Instead, they were more often scolded for mistakes or even subjected to harsh punishments. It was a time when parenting commonly involved direct criticism and inducing shame to enforce obedience.

Children who grow up knowing they are valued and that their very existence is a blessing likely have higher self-esteem. However, if you weren't one of those children, there's no need to blame your parents or the world. That was the norm back then, and most children were raised that way.

We often forget our own worth. While we know intellectually that everyone deserves recognition and love, when asked, "Do you think you are a cherished person?" many of us struggle to respond confidently. We understand that we should respect ourselves, yet we tend to believe that our value is dependent on the recognition and affection of others. However, self-worth does not require external validation.

Same Need for Recognition, Different Modes

In my counseling practice, I've noticed that many husbands who are dissatisfied with their marriages often suffer from low self-esteem. They feel undervalued by their wives. They desire to be seen as useful and important, but this need is frequently unmet. It's not hard to understand why. When problems arise, men tend to offer solutions. When their wives are having problems, they want to offer a great punch line of a solution and get credit for it. And when these efforts go unappreciated by their wives, it wounds their self-esteem. What these husbands want is simple: to feel that their wives see them as useful. Therein lies the husband's self-esteem. Conversely, a wife's self-esteem often hinges on having her feelings validated. When a husband shares in her feelings, marital satisfaction improves.

In couples therapy, one comes to learn just how important two people are to each other. Mature couples recognize that nurturing the partner's self-esteem is crucial for the health of their own self-esteem. They know they are in the same boat and that they live and die together.

This reflection on the subject of recognition brings to mind my first lecture at a conference. I was extremely nervous, and my legs shook as I stood at the podium. Despite being grateful for the opportunity, I was overwhelmed with self-doubt. I wasn't a university professor and had an unimpressive résumé. I feared being laughed at and wasting the audience's time. As I began speaking, my voice cracked and my hands shook. I worried that the audience would see that I was inexperienced. Then I heard a click. Someone was taking photos of my presentation. Over time, more cameras clicked. When I looked up, I saw people nodding and listening intently. Even elderly professors watched with interest. My tension eased and I regained my normal voice. That moment was when I felt acknowledged.

Before I took the stage, I was plagued by the question: *Do people need me here?* After all, there were many people at the conference who had studied more and had more experience than I did. Knowing that they would be listening to my lecture placed tremendous pressure on me, and I feared I would not have anything worthy to contribute.

This pressure slowed down my preparation for the lecture. I had to prepare alone after work, but I couldn't focus. The materials seemed too outdated, and I had to fight doubts about whether my translations of the sources cited were correct. As time went on, my anxiety worsened. My lack of experience, insufficient preparation, and stress about potentially ruining the opportunity made me want to call it quits.

I thought I was worried about disappointing the audience, but that was just an excuse. In truth, I was entirely consumed with concerns for myself: What if people thought I was a fraud? What if someone yawned or looked bored? What if I messed up the presentation?

The Desire for Recognition

There are many professionals and successful individuals who, like me, harbor doubts and anxieties about their abilities and achievements. People who excelled in school from a young age, currently earn a good salary, and seem to lack for nothing in other aspects of life find themselves constantly anxious. Some can't fall asleep without a strong drink to take the edge off.

Many of these highly successful people are haunted by obsessions. Obsessions involve persistent, repetitive thoughts, many of which stem from childhood. Thoughts like *If I don't come first, I'm worthless* or *If I fail this exam, I'll get in trouble with my parents* are instilled in childhood by well-meaning, devoted parents to such an extent that these become obsessions. Of course, there are many cases where the children develop these obsessions all on their own without parental involvement.

The worry of never gaining recognition generates a

powerful driving force. Even now, I am driving myself with thoughts like *I must become a useful doctor who writes books that prove essential to readers.* The problem is that relying solely on this method has its limits in producing results. Besides the fact that we all have limits to the energy we can expend, such motivation turns into anxiety and builds pressure. In fact, while I was writing this book, the pressure of having to write a great book was so paralyzing that I couldn't write a single word for a while. With the burden of needing to write a good book weighing heavily on my shoulders, I even worried that the book would not sell.

Being driven by the need for recognition may be useful during school years. Many high school students apply themselves with the thought that their lives will be over if they don't get into college. But once we enter society, recognition loses its effectiveness as a motivator. There are no important exams or classroom teachers in real life. We have to deal with evaluations throughout the year and seek recognition from more than one or two individuals. Moreover, if we seek to curry the favor of one particular person, we may be accused of trying to get ahead through flattery.

Focus on the Process, Not Evaluation

There are no clear guidelines for how best to conduct oneself at the workplace. There's no guide telling us what, when, and how much to do to gain recognition. There are no clear grades, no popularity votes. Therefore, ascertaining one's own worth is difficult, and feeling worthwhile is even more challenging.

Most of us belong to multiple communities. If we obsess over being acknowledged at work, we might neglect our families. If we focus solely on being good parents, we might encounter problems at work. Striving for recognition from our spouses might lead to issues with our parents. Since our energy is limited, it's impossible to please everyone in every way.

So what should we do? The answer lies in the process. Immerse yourself in the process. The result comes later; the process is now. Focusing on the process means concentrating on what you can do today. If you want to get a job, think only about what you can do today to get it. If you want to go to a good university, the result will come on the day the acceptance or rejection letter arrives, but the process is your decision today whether or not to study. The result isn't within our control, nor is it part of the present.

People who focus on the process can concentrate on themselves in the present. When we give our best every day toward the goal and are satisfied with the effort we make, we are less likely to be crushed when the outcome is not favorable. We may not pass the test, but we will derive satisfaction from the fact that we learned a great deal during our preparation.

To answer the question *How much do I like myself?* one must focus on self-evaluation rather than evaluations from others. Coming back to my own story about lectures, the way I prepare for lectures and presentations has changed since that first nerve-racking experience. Nowadays I focus solely on myself. The same goes for writing books. I write not to seek approval from others but to record the observations I've made, so that I can refer back to it whenever I feel overwhelmed or so that my daughters can read it when they need to. Consequently, I've become much more immersed in my process than before.

Today's Exercise for Healthy Self-Esteem: Write Down Why You Are Reading This Book

By this point, some of you may feel like putting this book down, thinking, *How can reading a book change anything?* This is natural. Instead, consider how you want to use this book.

If you bought this book to boost your self-esteem, then think specifically about how you want to change. Setting realistic personal goals increases your chances of success. Consider a high school student who is asked, "Why do you study hard?" The ones who answer "to become a great person" or "to make my mom happy" are likely not great students. The ones who answer "so I can get into a great university and make a lot of money" are likely more motivated.

Write down the specific changes you hope to achieve by reading this book. The more concrete and realistic your answers are, the better. If you want to feel more at peace, think about what that peace will help you achieve. If you want to love yourself more, consider what you want to do with that newfound self-love. Be as specific as possible, whether it's improving your romantic relationships, processing your breakup in a healthy way, or avoiding resentment toward others. Write down as many answers as you wish.

Professions That Can Undermine Self-Esteem

I am content with my job. It's something I aspired to from a young age, and it's a profession many envy. However, considering the state of healthcare in Korea, it can be incredibly frustrating. Still, I can't imagine having this level of satisfaction with any other career. For me, there is no other profession that's more ethical, more stable, or better suited. Perhaps that's why I haven't given up halfway.

Like all of us, I sometimes feel disillusioned with my job. I once worked at a hospital where my colleagues were wonderful but the institution had to file for bankruptcy, and there were times I felt unfulfilled even though I was earning well.

What helped me get through those times was understanding the distinction between a workplace and a profession. They are different. You can dislike your workplace yet still love your profession. Likewise, your profession and your dreams are also two different things. While I am a doctor, I have never abandoned my dream of becoming a writer.

When you are having doubts about the value of what

you do, it's crucial to separate your profession, your work-place, and your dreams. Otherwise, you risk feeling dissat-isfied with all three.

Self-Esteem in the Younger Generation

Some older people claim that the times of dire poverty and hardship were the best. I thought that couldn't possibly be true, but I understand where it comes from, especially when I see young people struggling with career choices and job prospects. Life has become more convenient due to technological advances, but the benefits also bring with them challenges and confusion.

In the past, goals were simpler. The path to happi-ness was simply to have enough to live on and to be physi-cally well. Eating well, having somewhere to live, having children, and earning money was enough. Upward mobility through hard work was the ultimate goal, and it wasn't as difficult to accomplish as it is now.

Today, young people must consider their direction in life. Good grades and degrees from prestigious uni-versities don't guarantee happiness. Even after entering college, there's worry about student loans and finding a job. Getting into a big company is no longer a secure path, as job security isn't what it used to be. Despite what older generations say, hard work alone doesn't guarantee a happy life.

It's no wonder that people begin to have doubts about the direction they have chosen. They cannot help but wonder, *Is this path truly the one I envisioned? What is the meaning of doing this work here?*

In the past, such doubts typically arose only after reaching middle age, but nowadays, young people are grappling with these questions from an early age. Comforting words meant to offer perspective, such as *Everyone lives like this* or *You're doing just fine* or *At least you have a family that loves you* provide only limited solace.

We live in a confusing era. It's a world where saving your salary for decades won't allow you to buy a house, where it's hard to land the job you want despite thorough preparation, and where you can follow the manual perfectly yet still be reprimanded for crossing the wrong person. We find ourselves constantly wondering who we are, where we are, and whether what we are doing is truly our calling.

Nowadays, a wider demographic from college seniors to middle-aged people and older are looking for career options. No one these days can confidently say that one occupation or other is great. Even aspiring doctors, who have status and seem to have stable work, are no different. Students I occasionally meet bluntly ask, "Is being a psychiatrist a good fit for you?" "How much do you earn?" or "Do you regret your choice?" While such questions catch me off guard sometimes, I can understand their need to ask. After students make it through the tough medical school years for the financial stability it promises, it's disconcerting to hear that doctors top the list for bankruptcy filings. It appears the legal profession isn't much different, either. Despite years of preparation and the work required to pass the bar, many lawyers still struggle to find employment.

In the past, one's career path was mostly determined by the age of nineteen. Medical students became doctors, law students entered the legal field, and engineering students landed secure jobs at major corporations, going on to lead stable lives. A future career was synonymous with a job, and once you had that job, the rest of your career trajectory was smooth sailing.

But today, boundaries between jobs have collapsed. The distinction between professions has blurred. Dermatologists and surgeons sometimes perform the same tasks, and pharmacists' work overlaps with that of traditional medicine practitioners. Even in the same workplace, the roles of permanent and contract employees are not significantly different. In a world where anyone can do the work you're doing and sometimes even replace you, it's confusing whether you should feel satisfied with your job the way it is or be wary of the competition, or where you should draw the line for contentment.

Jobs That Can Damage Self-Esteem

We feel secure when we are satisfied with our jobs and workplaces. Being on the path we wanted and having financial stability would be ideal. However, there are many job situations that inevitably lower self-esteem. Many work arrangements induce uncertainty about one's choices, causing feelings of inadequacy and self-doubt. These issues are more often than not products of societal conditions or systems, but many people nonetheless end up blaming themselves and feeling guilty.

Know the Difference Between Job Satisfaction, Career Satisfaction, and Self-Satisfaction

One crucial thing to remember is that the workplace should not be romanticized. It can be a challenging environment. That's why we receive a salary, paid regularly and on schedule. If it weren't for the compensation, no one would stay. If the workplace were such a fun and nurturing place, we wouldn't need to be paid. We are paid for our work because our employers require our skills and want us to stay. Of course, there can be many moments of happiness at work, and we are sometimes lucky enough to have supportive colleagues who help us through tough times. But these moments cannot be relied upon for the source of our happiness. The ultimate happiness we seek in life cannot be exclusively found at work.

Many clients have unrealistic expectations about workplace life. I suspect this self-delusion helps them survive the tough job search process. They envision the workplace as somewhere to achieve their dreams, have successful careers, realize their potential, and experience beautiful moments of camaraderie among colleagues.

Having such a narrow, idealized view of the workplace is unrealistic. An understanding, fair department head cannot be guaranteed. Dreams, growth, self-realization, and notions of a "workplace family" created by the bosses should be treated with caution. The workplace is there to demand your work and provide compensation. Therefore, do not base your self-esteem purely on work.

I hope employees around the world can clearly distinguish between their job, their career, and their dreams. Like me, you might be satisfied with your career but unhappy with your current workplace. Conversely, you might dislike your career but enjoy your current workplace. However, you must separate your job from your life. We do not live to go to work. The workplace is not our entire life. Just because you're unhappy with your workplace doesn't mean you should be miserable in all other areas of life. Similarly, your professional success may not always mean you're living the life you want.

We don't live to go to work; we live for the life that comes after work. Life after work is just as much a part of our lives, and weekends are important, too. There is no need to bring the stress from work home or to carry unfinished tasks into your personal time. Dwelling on work problems for too long won't solve them, either. Work is just work. We often assign too much meaning to it. It is important to completely detach and clear our minds from work once in a while.

Today's Exercise for Healthy Self-Esteem: No Thinking About Work After Clocking Out

The workplace drains our energy. Our salary is essentially a monetary conversion of the time spent at work. The longer the work hours and the higher the workload intensity, the more energy we lose. There's only one solution: Turn off thoughts about work the moment you leave the office.

Once you clock out, free yourself from all work-related thoughts until you clock in the next day. If you must take a work-related call or see your boss after hours, keep it short. As soon as you hang up or part ways, switch off thoughts about work. Of course, this is easier said than done. People might criticize you, saying you don't understand the realities of a working person. However, this is possible with practice. It's actually normal to avoid work calls and directives after hours. People assume it's acceptable because you comply. If this issue makes you consider quitting, even contemplating that should happen during work hours paid for by the company.

CHAPTER 12

How Valuable Am I?

Research shows that many people who win large sums in lotteries or hit the jackpot in casinos often suffer from depression. While the sudden influx of money undoubtedly makes the winner ecstatic, this happiness does not necessarily translate into sustained self-esteem. On the contrary, many of those who unexpectedly come into large amounts of money actually experience a decline in self-esteem. What accounts for this phenomenon? An explanation might be that one criterion we use to evaluate our self-worth includes the question *How useful am I to society?*

To maintain healthy self-esteem, we need to believe that we are necessary to society—be it the small society of our family and local community, or our country and the world. This is why we crave praise from our parents during our formative years and feel a sense of fulfilment when we vote.

The World Turns Just Fine Without Me

My college life was filled with group activities. From morning classes to group practicals and experiments, I was constantly surrounded by peers and professors, leaving little time for solitude. To have some alone time, I would often travel alone over vacations. I would board the last bus from the terminal bound for the farthest place available. I would take a good long nap on the bus and wake up in cities like Ulsan, Pohang, or Jinju.

These journeys involved wandering from one city to another with no specific destination. The goal wasn't to eat at famous restaurants or go sightseeing—I just wanted to be alone. Aside from brief visits to friends or relatives, I spent most of the time away by myself.

Roaming around unfamiliar cities felt liberating. Everyone I encountered was a stranger, freeing me from the need to be emotionally invested or feign interest in others. After a day of solitude, I would feel a sense of calm gradually descend on my weary mind. Over time, I began to miss the people I cared about, those I genuinely wanted to socialize with. Eventually, I even thought about those I clashed with—people who envied, criticized, or used me. Although I didn't miss everyone, my feelings of resentment toward them would diminish as my loneliness deepened. It was a fascinating experience.

When the feelings of wanting to distance myself from others and the loneliness of being alone balanced out, I would find myself heading back to Seoul. Sometimes I felt the urge to return to Seoul as soon as I reached my travel destination.

I stopped traveling alone, not because of loneliness or longing for people, but due to a growing anxiety. The realization that the world didn't miss me when I was gone made me uneasy. The longer my trips, the more liberated I felt. But I also grew nervous and sometimes even felt a pang of sadness at realizing the world continued on just fine in my absence.

After graduating from college, becoming an intern and then a specialist, and living as a scholar and psychiatrist, I gradually found peace. I believe this came from the increasing number of people who sought me out.

Nowadays, with a constant stream of patients, conference presentations, and lectures, if I were to suddenly take off on a solo trip like I used to, I would probably be reported missing within a day. In truth, that's a rather comforting thought.

Success as a Way of Gaining Social Value

One can gauge a person's success by examining how much they are needed by society. Of course, a lottery winner can be considered successful in a way, but their success is strictly tied to money. It has nothing to do with their character or value. The same logic applies to why a company president is essential, whereas if an employee falls ill, someone else can replace them. But as one moves up the ranks or takes on important responsibilities, one becomes increasingly harder to replace. A person whose absence would cause major problems for many is what we call a successful person.

When self-esteem issues arise, the question *Am I needed in society?* often surfaces. Failing job interviews repeatedly can shake your self-esteem because it can feel as though you are not needed anywhere. Similarly, someone who is criticized at work or called "worthless" by their parents is unlikely to have high self-esteem.

Our social relationships and roles are closely tied to our emotions. Everyone wants to be noticed and seen as necessary. This is the foundation that makes social life possible.

The feeling that "society needs me" satisfies our social instincts because it provides a sense of reassurance that even if we face problems, society will support us. Conversely, being rejected by society or facing prolonged indifference increases our fear of isolation. While some might dismiss negative evaluations from others as just their opinion, most people internalize these negative perceptions, which contributes to lower self-evaluation.

Let us consider the family, the most basic unit of society. When someone feels unwanted in their family, their self-esteem takes a big hit. It's challenging for them to maintain self-esteem if they think, *Are my parents staying in an unhappy marriage because of me?* or *A child like me is practically useless.* No one can feel satisfied with themselves if they believe they are dispensable or that they have ruined the lives of other family members.

The Psychology of Infidelity

The need to be needed also applies to marriage. Feeling unnecessary in one's family or to one's spouse can undermine self-esteem. Long-term corporate workers often become adept at surviving in the workplace and resolving interpersonal conflicts. However, my experience shows that such individuals often feel less valued by their spouses or families. Consider a person who holds an important position at work but is largely ignored by their spouse. What if they were to come across someone at work who appreciates their worth and encourages them? Hearing compliments like "How do you get such amazing results even in difficult situations? You're incredible!" or "I always respect you; please teach me more" can make anyone feel great about themselves. If you are recognized as a valuable social entity, your self-esteem resonates accordingly. Those with "office wives" or "office husbands" often say that these individuals recognize the value in them that their spouses do not. When a spouse accuses them of being a workaholic, the office spouse bolsters their fragile self-worth.

Many people engaging in infidelity suffer from low self-esteem. Their infidelity is not because they are all inherently promiscuous or driven by excessive sexual desire. Instead, the instinct to be recognized by someone unconsciously leads them to seek outside validation of their worth that their families do not provide.

However, this does not mean I endorse affairs or cheating. No matter the reason, even if it's a desperate struggle to reclaim one's self-worth, infidelity cannot be justified. It's akin to wanting to earn money by going to a casino. The vast sums of money in a gambling den are not yours. Similarly, trying to regain your self-esteem through infidelity is a sad, ineffective endeavor.

My Identity Is Not Singular

People who are well aware of their social value do not define themselves by just one aspect of their lives. We are all someone's child, but we don't live solely for our parents. We have careers, but we were not born just for our work. Each of us is a child, a spouse, a parent, a worker, a member of a local community, a club member, a friend, a resident of a city, and a citizen of a nation.

Our self-esteem may dip when we step into some roles and identities as opposed to others. For example, someone might be a stern father but an exceptional husband, a mediocre employee but an outstanding leader in their hobby group. The point is that it's impossible to excel and satisfy everyone in every role.

Therefore, you shouldn't label yourself as worthless just because you fall short in one particular role. If you don't shine as an employee, it doesn't mean you should condemn your entire self as worthless. Similarly, if your efforts to be a good daughter-in-law go unacknowledged, it doesn't mean you have no worth as a member of society. Even if you falter in one or two areas, you still remain a partner, friend, parent, volunteer, member of a religious group, or citizen. Failing to feel validated in one area doesn't mean you have to feel unwanted in all areas of life.

Today's Exercise for Healthy Self-Esteem: Reflect on Your Various Identities and Roles

Most of us become members of a family from the moment we are born. As we grow, our social spheres expand. We become members of schools and workplaces. Look at the range of environments you belong to now and think about how you can become a valuable person within them.

Examples

Family member: *Engage in conversations, greet your family warmly.*

Neighbor: *Help others shovel snow.*

Employee: *Avoid being late to work, increase productivity.*

Religious Community Member: *Practice your faith, join community groups.*

Citizen: *Participate in elections, attend rallies, support politicians.*

Alumni Association Member: *Organize and attend alumni gatherings.*

Sports team member: *Help arrange social functions outside of training sessions.*

CHAPTER 13

Overcoming Indecisiveness

Making good decisions boosts self-esteem. However, people with low self-esteem often struggle to make even the simplest choices because they don't trust themselves. When faced with conundrums, we tend to seek out someone trustworthy for advice, hoping they'll understand us best. Whether or not they are helpful is secondary; simply sharing our worries makes us feel better and seems to provide solutions.

But if there's one person who is always present and ready to listen, it's ourselves. Trusting ourselves makes life easier. We won't need to constantly seek out others for advice or worry about revealing our vulnerabilities. By consulting with ourselves, finding solutions, and affirming our choices with a *Well done, you did great,* we become our best advisors.

Three Conditions for Making Good Decisions

Adulthood is a series of decisions, big and small. From choosing schools, colleges, universities, careers and partners, life is a learning process of continuous decision-making. When faced with choices, whom do we turn to? We often look at how others have chosen in similar situations, studying the paths of others as we try to make the best decisions and avoid regrets later. The reason many seek others' advice is simple: Doing as others do feels safe and ensures at least average results. Yet some problems only we can solve. A wise counselor offers options and reminds the client that "the decision is ultimately yours to make."

Making wise decisions independently is a mark of maturity. So what does it mean to make good decisions? Here are three key points to consider. The first is timeliness. Even the right decision loses value if it's delayed too long. Those with decision paralysis often overlook this, postponing the task for a perfect, regret-free choice. Wise decision-makers keep their deadlines. The second is knowing the scope of the decision. Any decision, no matter how wise, must be within the realm of one's control. We cannot decide for others or foresee the future. For example, students often ask, "Which medical school is better, Harvard or NYU?" But this decision is premature if they haven't even started studying. Decisions should focus on what options are available to us right now. The third is knowing that there is no perfect decision. In the moment of the decision, we cannot know for certain if we will come to regret it later. What seems the best decision might lead to regrets, and hastily made choices could turn into blessings. Only time reveals outcomes, and life is full of surprises. Good decision-makers bear this in mind and understand that there's no universal right answer, and it's the follow-through that matters more than the choice itself. They don't waste energy over the decision-making process.

Good decision-makers have the power to be content with their choices. They remain unaffected by casual remarks from third parties, unsolicited advice, or jealousy-fueled criticisms. Because they have a strong inner compass, their decisions tend to be sound and logical, avoiding reckless choices masked as confidence.

The Neuroscience of Right Decisions

The process of making correct decisions blends emotion and reason. When making a choice, we use our knowledge and judgment to arrive at a decision, then lend emotional support to this decision. Good decision-makers neither stubbornly defend their choices nor fret that they might have made the wrong choice.

Scientifically, this balance involves the frontal lobe, responsible for rationality, and the limbic system, which governs emotions. Problems arise when one dominates the other. Purely rational decisions that do not take into account how we feel about them cannot be considered wise. Conversely, solely emotional decisions lack practicality. Hence, for balanced decisions, both the frontal lobe and limbic system must be engaged. Ignoring the emotional impact a decision might have on others, even if a decision seems right, is not wise. Decisions that completely ignore social contracts and customs are not sustainable.

Overly emphasizing positivity can also lead to poor

decisions. Addiction-prone individuals make quick, regret-free decisions, propelled by false confidence and instant gratification. People who make reckless investments have deluded themselves into thinking it is wise to invest their life savings in a high-risk stock. Shopaholics also derive a false sense of satisfaction from buying things they convince themselves they need. Feeling good about a decision does not make a decision sound. Good decisions are based on a balanced mix of reason and emotion.

People Deprived of the Opportunity to Make Decisions

Unfortunately, Korean society tends to overemphasize rational judgment. I believe this issue stems from an intensely competitive culture and a strong focus on education.

Even before children start school, they are busy searching for the right answers. Instead of thinking things through and forming their own opinions, they are preoccupied with finding the correct answer to fill in the blanks. In school, the emphasis is on solving math and science problems correctly, leaving little room for children's thoughts or feelings. Through this process, children unknowingly become accustomed to choosing rational answers. They grow up believing that ignoring emotions and being indifferent to others' feelings are necessary to succeed in a competitive environment.

Adults often instruct children what the answers are and

tell them to memorize the answers without giving them a chance to think over the problems on their own, thus depriving them of the opportunity to make decisions and develop decision-making skills. We frequently witness the adverse effects of this kind of education. Among the so-called exam geniuses who pass notoriously difficult exams from a young age, some are labeled as "exam psychopaths."

The limbic system is a crucial part of the brain that needs to be nurtured. While the development of the pre-frontal cortex, which aids us in studying well, is crucial, the ability to reflect on and empathize with emotions is equally important. This balance is essential for developing the ability to make decisions. Furthermore, compared to the prefrontal cortex, which continues to develop into one's twenties and thirties, the limbic system matures much earlier.

Therefore, children need to develop the habit of making decisions by themselves from a young age. Adults should not make decisions for children out of fear that they might regret them later or blame bad decisions on the parents. It's vital to train children to use both limbic system and prefrontal cortex harmoniously from a young age. Nevertheless, a lack of decision-making experience in childhood doesn't mean one will live with poor decision-making skills forever. There are ways to develop these skills later in life, so there's no need to be discouraged.

Ways to Improve Decision-Making Skills

As previously mentioned, good decision-making means having a balance between rationality and emotion. In other words, both the prefrontal cortex and the limbic system need to be well-activated and interact smoothly. Here are some methods to help enhance decision-making skills.

Engage in Art

The process of harmoniously activating the prefrontal cortex and the limbic system often occurs during artistic activities. Art frequently involves expressing emotions. However, simply expressing feelings randomly doesn't make it art. The prefrontal cortex must be engaged to find the best way to express these emotions. An artist must calculate what kind of painting to create and what colors to use, while a writer must decide what and how to write. This process naturally improves decision-making skills. Children are encouraged to take art and music classes from an early age for this reason.

Make a Decision Scale

When deciding whether to do something, you can create a decision scale. A decision scale weighs the pros and cons of taking an action against those of not taking it. People tend to be influenced by emotions before making a decision.

Objectively expressing these emotions can reveal what truly matters. Using a decision scale helps make abstract emotions clearer.

Writing things down and placing them on a decision scale can clarify the nature of the decision you need to make. For example:

	To Drink	Not to Drink
Pros	Relieve stress. Feel good.	Better for liver. Improved relationship with partner.
Cons	Tired the next day. Weight gain and other negative impacts on health.	Life gets boring. Hard to socialize without drinking.

Dividing Wants and Needs

Nowadays, many young people say they don't know what to do. On the other hand, perhaps influenced by self-help books that advise young people to "dream big," many feel overwhelmed by the wealth of options. Having many wants is good, but it's problematic if one dreams without doing what needs to be done. Spending too much time thinking about what to do can lead to inaction. In such cases, it helps to distinguish between what you want to do and what you must do.

What I Want to Do: Learn Japanese. Date. Perform well
at work.

What I Need to Do: Prepare for tomorrow morning's
presentation.

This distinction makes it clear what needs to be done
right now.

Doing Both

You don't always have to choose between wants and needs.
Find the intersection between the two. For example, if you
need to prepare for a presentation, this doesn't mean you
have to give up everything else. Turn the presentation into
an opportunity to perform well at work. Especially when
you are facing a crossroads in your career, such as choosing
between becoming a writer and finding a job, you can work
during the week and write on weekends. Alternatively, you
can write blog posts related to your job.

Today's Exercise for Healthy Self-Esteem: Write and Draw Your Points of Conflict

To strengthen self-esteem, you need to make good
decisions, starting with small ones. Small decisions accumulate to form significant decisions, and the better you
handle important decisions, the more your self-esteem
will grow.

Express your current points of conflict as follows:

Example 1

Option A: Go to sleep now.
Option B: Eat ramen instead.

Example 2

Option A: Go to sleep now.
Option B: Call ex instead.

By writing down your conflicts, you can see clearly what you need to deliberate on. Then you can choose one of the two options. If the answer isn't immediately apparent, list the pros of both options side by side.

Example 1

Option A: Go to sleep now. I'll wake up feeling good tomorrow morning.
Option B: Eat ramen instead. I'll feel full and satisfied now.

Example 2

Option A: Go to sleep now. I won't regret it tomorrow morning.
Option B: Call ex instead. If I'm lucky, I'll get to hear their voice.

Laying it out makes it clear which is the better decision. I would choose to go to sleep. I hope you came to the same conclusion.

CHAPTER 14

Why Reading Self-Help Books Doesn't Improve Self-Esteem

Two years ago, when I received the news of my grand-mother's passing, my first thought was *This marks the end of my childhood.* It also meant that the only remaining person in the world who called me "my grandson" had departed this world. My grandparents have always been special to me. While I was growing up, whenever my self-esteem plummeted and I felt discouraged, it was my grandparents who helped me endure those moments. Sometimes I fool myself into thinking I have become successful on my own, but when I picture their faces, I must admit how fortunate I've been to have their support. Perhaps it is due to this gratitude and sense of regret that I feel particularly sympathetic toward those who had an unhappy childhood, were constantly bullied by adults, or cannot remember anything from their childhood at all.

Childhood Memories as Emotional Scars

In the American TV series *Desperate Housewives*, there is a character named Bree. She appears to have everything: a lovely home in a quiet town, a physician for a husband. Her house is beautiful, impeccably organized, and every evening a grand dinner is prepared on the large dining table. All the household items are polished and cleaned as if she is running a high-end hotel.

However, her family is not happy. Her husband and children suffer from a lack of affection. Despite this, there doesn't seem to be anything particularly wrong with her. She prepares vegetarian meals for her husband to lower his cholesterol and teaches her children sound moral principles and values.

Yet her husband finds her robotic and feels lonely and powerless even when he's with her. Her middle school daughter seeks the love she doesn't get from her parents through an inappropriate relationship with a teacher. Despite their seemingly perfect exterior, there is a palpable tension and stress within this family.

It has been a long time since I watched this drama, but Bree's family stuck with me because I encounter many clients who had similar upbringings. They have mothers with obsessive behaviors, fathers who are passive, and a household filled with frequent arguments and a cold, perennial tension that leaves wounds and unresolved issues.

If a person's unhappy childhood is imprinted on their body and mind, they are likely to perceive themselves negatively. We tend to search for reasons and outcomes for everything. Once someone labels themselves as a child of divorced parents, a son raised by a violent father, or the child of an unhappy home, it becomes difficult to respect oneself.

Psychological Dependence on Psychology

People who had a difficult upbringing tend to worry a lot. They unconsciously know that past experiences influence their present life, especially if that unhappiness stemmed from their family and continues to affect them.

Their worries often reflect their parents' behaviors. Someone raised by parents who often fought might fear they won't manage their own marriage well. Those who grew up with violent parents might worry about becoming abusers or victims of violence themselves. Children of alcoholics or gambling addicts might fear becoming addicts themselves or marrying an addict. They continue to harbor doubts that they can ever experience love or marriage with such emotional baggage.

Those who actively seek to work on these issues often read various psychology or self-help books. They want to understand how people who were unhappy and hurt managed their lives, and they want to seek solutions. These books offer a wealth of information and answers, helping many people. The books help readers identify their emotions and understand their causes through academic insights. People who find comfort and support in self-help books generally go through the following stages.

Universalization

The realization that "I'm not the only one like this" is powerful. People who thought they were unique in their unhappy circumstances find solace in knowing that there are many others who've had it worse. This realization lightens their hearts and offers comfort.

Relief from Guilt

Self-help books describe numerous factors that contribute to a person's issues, explaining that these problems mostly aren't due to personal failings or incompetence. These persuasive explanations lead to the realization that the reader is not to blame, helping them unload the guilt they've been carrying around for ages. They come to understand that their struggles aren't due to a lack of willpower or immaturity, but rather are a natural response to their experiences.

Acquiring Knowledge

Understanding and interpreting emotions rationally bring peace of mind. Recognizing that their struggles were due to long-standing trauma, identifying core emotions that dominated their lives, and learning that their parents used projection as a defense mechanism, for instance, help readers with difficult childhoods make sense of their painful experiences. What felt like a foggy emotional landscape becomes clearer. Situations that once required days of venting to friends can be succinctly summarized in a few sentences, making emotional recovery much easier.

Restoring Self-Esteem Is Like
Getting into Shape

Wouldn't it be great if reading a few self-help books could solve all our problems? The issue, however, lies in the fact that each book offers different instructions. Reading self-help books indiscriminately, following their guidelines, and attending famous lectures often lead to greater frustration rather than improvement. In extreme cases, people might conclude, *Since nothing seems to work no matter how hard I try, I must be fundamentally incurable,* leading to a sense of hopelessness.

Nevertheless, the very attempt to seek out these books in order to identify and resolve issues deserves to be applauded. If you have delved into your mind and tried solutions that might help, your mind is undoubtedly on the path to recovery. However, the process of mental recovery takes time and sometimes involves returning to square one, just as going on a diet doesn't result in immediate weight loss. You might lose some weight only to regain it, and you could even cause damage to other parts of your body if you are not careful. This is why I compare the process of restoring self-esteem to getting into shape.

In that sense, those who only read self-help books are akin to those who only read bodybuilding manuals. A training manual might explain why the body is out of shape and how to build muscles. However, theory without practice is just knowledge. To get into shape, you need to sweat and work out your muscles. The same goes for self-esteem. Reading self-help books alone and expecting change is like saying, "I read a lot of fitness books, but I still haven't lost weight!"

I'm often surprised by how many self-taught psychology enthusiasts harbor significant resentment toward their parents. They uniformly attribute their problems to their parents. Rationalizing their issues and confining them to problems in their upbringing is the easiest solution. They readily believe that their past, particularly their parents, made them who they are and conclude that the future will be no different. It's truly unfortunate.

Memories Evoke Emotions

This may sound self-evident, but being trapped in unhappy memories generates negative emotions. When caught in negative emotions, only the negative events of the past come to mind. If there were any occasional happy memories, they do not surface.

This phenomenon is especially evident in couples who have been fighting for a long time. Unhappy couples frequently use words like *always, never,* and *every day*—"He always lies to me"; "She nags me every day, so I have to get out of the house"; and so forth—in their complaints.

The reason is that using these words makes it easier to label the past negatively. They conclude with statements like "I've never been happy with you!" and shut out any good memories. From a scientific perspective, this is a very natural reaction. The hippocampus, which governs memory, and the amygdala, which governs emotions, are connected in our brain. Hence, when you're sad, you tend to recall sad events, and when you're resentful, you tend to remember only the resentful events of the past.

What this translates to is that when we are tormented by certain past experiences, we need to check in with ourselves to see if we are experiencing any emotional issues. It may not be that one is depressed because of sad memories, but that sad memories keep surfacing because one is depressed. And when one is constantly revisited by sad memories, one's self-esteem suffers.

Keeping a Distance from Your Unhappy Past or Letting It Go Altogether

Living with a painful past is not easy. It's like living with a ball of fire in your chest. When your self-esteem is healthy, the fire is a safe source of heat that keeps you warm. But when your self-esteem is low, it turns into a dangerous weapon that burns you.

The size and intensity of the flame vary from person to person. However, depending on how much distance you can put between yourself and those past experiences, your self-esteem can be protected or reduced to ashes.

Many people with strong self-esteem have had unhappy pasts. They also feel pain and self-pity when recalling their past. However, the feelings do not linger. Such people know how to keep their distance from the memories of the past. Through self-reflection and coping tools, they have come to understand that painful memories are in the past.

Conversely, people with low self-esteem carry their unhappiness around on their chest or shoulders. They keep bringing up their unhappy past at every turn, being scalded and wounded again each time rather than letting the past fade away. Not content with just that, they show their past to everyone they meet. When they develop feelings for someone, they rush to share stories of being abused by their parents or bullied by peers, seeking empathy or testing if the other person can handle their baggage. They transfer the fire in their hearts to their coworkers or romantic interests.

All pain is in the past. We must not forget this. Reversing time is beyond human power. Between the painful past and the present, we have the gift of time. This gift is given equally to everyone. Why reject this gift? Shouldn't we gratefully accept it?

Imagine a Different Past and Plan for the Future

Of course, most of us are aware that the past is in the past, but it's not easy to escape the hold our memories have on us. Despite all our efforts to forget and let go, how can we stop these painful memories from replaying before our eyes? When the past wounds do not stay in the past but keep erupting in the present, more proactive methods are needed to let go of the past.

Ask Yourself "What If?"

How would you be living now if it weren't for your unhappy past? For example, if your parents had a bad relationship but it had no impact on you now, how would you have turned out differently? Ask yourself what your life would look like today if the constant criticisms you received in your childhood had not affected you. Answers will emerge, such as *If I wasn't affected by it, I would have gotten over the breakup sooner,* or *I wouldn't be wallowing in self-pity, calling myself a lousy mom.*

Set Goals for the Future

People who dwell on the past often fail to think about the present or future because they're preoccupied with why they can't change. Now it's time to set goals. The goals should be positive, outlined in the future tense, and centered around actions rather than emotions. For example, if you've broken up with your partner, the goal shouldn't be *I don't want to have any regrets* (negative) but rather *I'll get over it one day* (positive). Instead of *Don't get irritated by mother-in-law's interference* (emotion-based, negative), the goal should be *Exercise for thirty minutes on days she stresses me out* (action-based, positive). Goals should be future-oriented, positive, and action-focused.

When the Alternative Is Impossible to Imagine

For some, it may be impossible to ask themselves "What if?" Some have been bound to the past or emotions surrounding the negative experiences for too long, while others have too powerful a craving for the sympathy or pity their misfortune attracts. These people ought to take the time to build this ability.

If You Can't Escape the Thought
That You'll Never Change

If you find yourself thinking, *I'll never escape my past. I'll never change!* this is a good place to start. Honest confrontation of your current state is the starting point for change. The past is not inescapable; it only seems that way when you are so bogged down in your negative experiences and emotions that you cannot find the headspace for solving the problem. With practice in controlling emotions and distancing yourself from a few bad habits, you can break free from the belief that change is impossible.

Today's Exercise for Healthy Self-Esteem: Ask "What If?" and Set Goals

Imagine what your life would look like today if you were not influenced by past experiences. Then write down future-oriented, positive, and action-based goals for that imagined life.

For example:

If my parents had had a harmonious relationship, how would I have turned out differently?

I would believe that I could also have a good marriage and would live without rejecting the idea of marriage.

If my father's business hadn't failed when I was in high school, how would I have turned out differently?

I wouldn't have wasted my twenties resenting my father. I would live pursuing what I wanted to do, unburdened by my family's financial problems.

CHAPTER 15

Seeing Myself as Too Different

Everyone wants to excel at building and maintaining relationships, but it's not that easy. Forming human connections is much like driving on a busy highway: No matter how skilled or cautious you are, an accident can still occur if you happen to have reckless drivers around you. You need to be good, but your efforts alone aren't enough.

Those with low self-esteem often assume that any issues in their relationships stem from their own faults. This mindset leads to guilt, which hinders healthy relationship-building. Lacking confidence, they either depend excessively on others or become defensive out of fear of rejection, which in turn negatively impacts the relationships. When you devalue yourself, it's hard to devise solutions because guilt and self-blame cloud your judgment.

Different Isn't Bad

Universalization is a therapeutic technique that helps clients realize their struggles and pain are not unique to them. Just knowing that many others face similar issues can be reassuring. Conversely, believing you're alone in your struggles makes the burden even harder to bear. Not only do you suffer from the ordeal itself, but the loneliness and feeling of isolation add to the pain.

This is why people often find solace in groups with shared experiences, where they can exchange stories and find comfort in knowing there are others experiencing the same strife. This shared understanding can provide the energy needed to overcome adversity.

Artists or people with strong artistic sensibilities often come seeking help, frustrated by their sensitive, perceptive natures. "I wish I were more like others. I wish I were a robot that never gets angry or cries," some say. They seem to believe that it is shameful to let one's emotions show and that they are weak and lack self-control. Upon delving into their past, they often discover that they've been chastised since childhood for being overly sensitive or, in the case of men, unmanly. These individuals carry two misconceptions: first, that they are different from others, and second, that being different is bad. This logic leads to the conclusion that they are worse than others.

Being different is not bad at all. There is nothing wrong with being sensitive, and being in tune with one's emotions is a valuable trait. You can quickly pick up on others' emotional shifts and have a keen sense of cultural trends. Such characteristics, however, can worry parents. I can see how parents might misunderstand frequent tears as a lack of self-confidence or too much laughter as a lack of seriousness.

When we write off our characteristics as bad, we come

to believe that we aren't deserving of empathy. We don't reveal our true feelings for fear that we will be criticized rather than understood. We stay on the periphery of social groups, finding it hard to open up, and are reluctant to connect with others. At the other extreme, even having too many admirable qualities can hinder close connections.

You Are Not Uniquely Miserable

People plagued by their difficult pasts often feel uniquely cursed. They hide their experiences out of shame, believing their lives are just too strange. This can apply to people who had a difficult relationship with their parents, experienced prolonged exposure to being criticized, or who grew up separated from family. People with such backgrounds tend to conceal their pasts and idealize others' lives.

Cultural norms that romanticize the notion of family and place emphasis on its importance exacerbate this issue. For instance, the myth of the all-sacrificing mother perpetuates unrealistic expectations. Constant media portrayals of perfect family dinners make individuals believe everyone else grew up in such loving homes.

The realization that one's upbringing was different from the norm often hits in adulthood, especially upon entering college. Leaving the neighborhood one grew up in and encountering diverse backgrounds and seeming disparities magnify this feeling. Many college students struggle to adapt, partly due to this psychological burden. They see other well-adjusted and sociable students who seem to come from well-to-do families with loving parents and assume they had easy childhoods.

Talking with a close friend often resolves these feelings. Hearing that you're not alone and that others went through similar stuff can be immensely comforting. Shared experiences allow one to communicate and bond. However, some may further isolate themselves, convinced their lives are unusually troubled. They miss opportunities for empathy.

When someone believes that their misfortunes are unique, it's difficult to convince them otherwise. Misery's impact isn't relative. Some may suffer all their lives over what seems a minor issue to others, while others show unusual resilience in recovering from more severe traumas. If someone believes in their unique misery, they may well have a reason to do so. Remember, their distress is deeper than it appears to an outsider.

The "Why Me?" Mentality

When thoughts like *Why just me?* take root, negative self-perception is combined with irrational emotional distress. *Why* adds blame, making the individual resent their life and fate.

Human memory is inherently unstable and tends to fade over time. However, *Why me?* links memory with emotion, making it harder to forget. These thoughts repeatedly bring bad memories and emotions to the surface, hindering the natural process of forgetting.

To let go of bad experiences, avoid linking them to

emotions. Stop asking *Why me?* or *Why am I like this?* These questions trigger bad memories and feelings, exacerbating isolation and a tendency to shy away from relationships.

Today's Exercise for Healthy Self-Esteem: Identify and Share Your Unique Traits

The first step toward change is awareness. Knowing how you perceive your uniqueness is crucial. Today, list what you believe makes you different. Include any painful aspects of your upbringing, parents, or experiences. Then share your list with a trusted friend or supporter, saying, "I think these aspects make me different. What do you think?"

What Makes Me Different from Others:

My Friend's Opinion:

CHAPTER 16

Understanding the Psychology of the Self-Conscious

Why me? is an expression of resentment. You may find yourself blaming your parents, your own actions, society, certain groups of people, or even harboring anger toward a higher power. If these thoughts are turned inward, they become self-criticism. Feeling inadequate can bring a sense of shame. When you believe you're the only one struggling with something everyone else seems to handle with ease, a profound sense of worthlessness can follow.

Many people struggle with the feeling that they aren't as level-headed or composed as others in their social interactions. They see others as being self-assured and independent, while they themselves feel overly sensitive and awkward. This might stem from the strong emphasis on individualism in modern society. It seems like others can maintain a perfect balance between personal space and social interaction, drifting farther away from those who feel they are constantly fettered to others' judgment. This leads to the recurring thought: *Why am I the only one who cares so much about what others think?*

Caring or Self-Conscious?

Consider a caring college student. He was always the first to help classmates with their difficulties, often taking on challenging tasks. Post-graduation, he became an exemplary employee—efficient, polite, considerate. His dedication was unmatched. He came in on weekends to cover his coworkers' shifts at the last minute, pulled late nights, and never whined, complained, or got angry. He was, by all accounts, the perfect employee.

However, not everyone liked him. His girlfriend, in particular, found him exasperating. She would often say accusingly, "You're not kind. You're just afraid that others won't like you!" When the couple came to me with this issue, the girlfriend insisted that the boyfriend wasn't being helpful but was simply desperate to be liked; if he were genuinely nice, he would not habitually break his plans with his girlfriend to help someone else.

Initially, the man rejected his girlfriend's criticism, convinced she was just being jealous and demanding. He said they could not talk this out and that he was sick of having the same arguments. He was seriously considering breaking up with her and confessed this wasn't the first time he'd broken up with someone over the same issue.

But over time, he began to see a grain of truth in her words. Reflecting on his childhood, he recalled his parents constantly urging him to be kind and help others, accompanied by the admonition, *What will people think if you don't?* He realized that his behavior, motivated by a desire to please others and avoid conflict, often neglected his own needs and those of his loved ones.

Why Excessive Kindness Is Looked Down On

Kindness is a virtue. A kind person is generally well liked. But it is important to ask yourself if you are being kind at your own expense. The boyfriend, initially rejecting his girlfriend's views, began to see that the problem was with him. Her claim that he was always focused on others seemed increasingly valid, the more he thought about it.

He was just behaving as his parents had taught him to, but the partners he cherished couldn't endure it and eventually left him. This man was good to others but not to himself. He did not care about his own time, happiness, or interests. These tendencies often lead to neglecting not just oneself but also those close to you.

This explains why someone who is a great friend might be distant with their romantic partners. They equate their partner with themselves and thus fail to give the partner attention. Think of the patriarchal grandfather in TV dramas—extremely kind and caring to neighbors or relatives, yet strict with his own children. This stems from the misapplication of the credo "Generous toward others, strict with yourself." What did his loved ones do to deserve this treatment?

In modern society, people who put others first with little regard for themselves are often looked down on.

We subconsciously perceive excessively kind people in a negative light. They may seem insincere. We wonder if we are about to be conned or if we would be forced to return the favor somehow, and we tend to think that overly kind people might have ulterior motives.

This is why model students in schools are sometimes ignored, and hardworking or overly nice colleagues aren't always popular at work. Excessive kindness, no matter how well intentioned, is not always interpreted kindly, especially in a workplace where competition is implicit. The harder one works, the more likely others will think, *You're making the rest of us look bad.*

Of course, no one openly berates someone for being nice, as that would be poor form. But people still want to belittle their actions and intentions. This impulse is in itself a sort of self-defense mechanism.

The Secret of the Popularity of the Aloof Person

This explains why nice people can struggle with relationships, particularly in the workplace. They put in so much effort and get little in return. People seem grateful, but the nice colleague becomes increasingly isolated at work and feels unjustly punished for working hard.

Problems also arise at home. Someone who cares too much about others' opinions is in danger of becoming a workaholic. To protect the family, they believe they must earn money, leading to voluntary overtime. However, the devoted parent is not spared from falling into this trap, either. Obsessing over providing the best food and education for their children and worrying that their children might come to resent them for not giving them the best possible care can result in very little time or space for self-care.

When we view our family as an extension of ourselves, we often make the mistake of prioritizing the needs and opinions of neighbors and acquaintances over those of family members. This leads to parents frequently saying to their children, "What would people say?" This habit of prioritizing others' opinions over one's own emotions is passed down through generations. Children who grow up hearing this become sensitive to the judgment of others, unable to prioritize their own feelings or desires. They may appear outwardly kind, but their mental and emotional health suffer.

Protagonists in TV shows these days are often depicted as aloof. These characters, who are far from kind and show little interest in the feelings of others, focusing solely on their own wishes, are extremely popular. Why? Because they are attractive. Confident people who value their tastes, pay attention to their emotions, and hold themselves in high regard are attractive. People admire those who are true to themselves no matter what others think.

There was a time when being considerate was a virtue. This was true in an agrarian society, where cooperation was vital for farming and caring for others was akin to caring for oneself. However, our society has become more divided and diversified over time, and values have shifted. Being considerate by old standards can be perceived as overstepping or meddling these days. The efforts to be considerate may be seen as being overly cautious or self-conscious. As society changes, so do values.

Embracing Selfish Altruism

The question of whether to live for oneself or for others is a delicate one. However, I often tell people, "Put yourself first." Sometimes, I advise quite bluntly, "Make selfish decisions and follow through with them," because I believe this is the natural way to behave.

I believe that it is human nature to be positively selfish. Recognizing and accepting this is the mature thing to do. Being kind and caring while also being positively selfish in pursuing one's needs and wants is natural, yet we sometimes assume these approaches to be mutually exclusive of one another. For many, they go hand in hand. Of course, there are many people who live a life of service to others. Why do they help others? Because it brings them joy. They continue to help because it makes them happy. I respect those who volunteer for their maturity, because it takes a wise person to understand the profound joy of helping others and to derive true happiness from it.

Parental love for one's children works the same way. Parents want their children to be happy. When their children smile, parents are happy, too. So parents keep doing things that make their children happy because it also makes them happy.

When we engage in acts of kindness solely for the happiness of others, it can lead to feelings of betrayal and resentment when we do not feel thanked or acknowledged for our nice deeds. Serve others for your own satisfaction and love your children because loving them brings you joy. Only then will there be no regrets or lingering feelings of resentment, and you will be able to love unconditionally and truly care for others.

Today's Exercise for Healthy Self-Esteem: Write Down What You Want

People who have been overly concerned with others' opinions often do not have a strong sense of who they are. They lose touch with who they are and what they like or dislike. As a result, they can't tell if their desires align with their actions.

Starting now, write down specifically what you want. This can include what you want from others or what you want for yourself. As you write, you might find that you're listing others' desires rather than your own. But don't worry about that. Look at your list of what you want and start taking an interest in yourself. If your list includes things others want from you, simply acknowledge that you really do care a lot about what others think.

When describing what you want, write sentences that meet these three criteria: (a) positive, not negative statements, (b) subject-oriented, with "I" as the subject, (c) future-oriented, not past-oriented.

For example:

Instead of "I don't want to feel anxious anymore" (negative), write: "I want to feel at ease" (positive).

Instead of "I want others to love me" (others as subject), write: "I want to be confident in myself" (*I* as subject).

Instead of "I used to be timid and lazy" (past), write: "I want to become bold and diligent" (future).

CHAPTER 17

Overly Dependent People

Dependence is a term as varied and nuanced as *self-esteem.* People interpret it differently, yet it almost always carries a negative connotation. Our society often values the *independent* person and sees them as the ideal and healthy.

However, is dependence truly a vice and is independence always virtuous? Is leaning on others truly problematic in a world that is becoming tougher to navigate?

Certainly, overdependence can be an issue, but in this chapter, we will explore what healthy dependence looks like and how outcomes can differ based on what or whom we depend on, and we'll provide guidance on distinguishing between healthy and unhealthy dependencies.

We Were All Dependent Once

Every baby is dependent. They cannot survive without their mother. A newborn cannot even hold its head up to nurse, let alone crawl. It is no wonder that babies feel anxious when separated from their mothers.

This dependency is not just about physical needs like being fed and changed. Babies have trouble putting themselves to sleep without being held and sung to by their parents. When babies begin to develop emotions, they need the parents' help with regulating them as well. Remnants of this dependency remain into adulthood. Teenagers and adults alike seek companionship for this reason. They prefer not to be alone and seek out someone to share their innermost thoughts with. Love and attachment are remnants of dependent behavior developed in one's infancy, which is why it is natural for adults to depend on others as well. Some maintain their juvenile attachment to their mothers, but most form new attachments with friends, partners, mentors, or religion, and in less ideal cases, with drugs or alcohol.

Life often boils down to how we manage our dependencies. There are immature, indiscriminate forms of dependence, and then there are sophisticated, healthy dependencies.

Unhealthy Dependence

Dependence is an instinct. Dependence is essential for survival in infancy, and as we grow into adulthood, the way we manage our dependence matures.

There are three main types of unhealthy dependence: overdependence, misplaced dependence, and denial of one's dependence.

Individuals who are overly dependent cannot tolerate being alone and are anxious about being excluded from their peer groups. These individuals might rush into new relationships immediately after a breakup or even have overlapping relationships to avoid being alone. A senior employee might seek solace from a junior colleague, or a professor might lean on a student for emotional support. Such inappropriate dependence is problematic. Those who form healthy dependence, on the other hand, seek support from appropriate sources rather than take advantage of relationship dynamics.

Most people with unhealthy dependence styles are unaware of or refuse to acknowledge their dependence. For example, parents who say, "I just want my child to be happy," are unconsciously revealing their dependence. This can burden the child, making them feel responsible for their parents' happiness, leading to confusion between their own desires and their parents' expectations.

Unhealthy dependence can also have a negative impact on relationships with spouses or partners. When relationships are strained, partners often blame each other. One of them might believe they would be happier and saner if only their partner would change. This reveals a subconscious belief that one's happiness depends on one's partner. Those who form unhealthy dependence may depend on people they claim not to trust. Rather than relying on a dependable person they respect and admire, who can give them the support they need, they demand support from those who can't and then resent them for it. In psychology terms, this is known as projection, where a person deflects their issues onto others, such as blaming their unhappiness on a child's failure or a disappointing spouse. Whether or not the child or spouse is actually at fault is irrelevant;

one cannot be happy when one continues to depend on people who cannot deliver and who cannot stop or even acknowledge the unhealthy dependence.

Healthy Dependence

People who form healthy dependence on others, first and foremost, are aware that they are relying on outside sources for support. High self-esteem doesn't mean handling everything alone. Instead, it involves recognizing one's limits and openly seeking help from others.

Here are three traits of mature dependence: dependence on capable entities, transparency, and reciprocation. People who form mature dependence know where to look for support. For knowledge, they turn to books; for health, they consult doctors. They depend on people and sources that can offer them what they need, and keep the relationship open and transparent, without resorting to secretive or harmful behaviors, as with alcohol or infidelity. Instead, they depend on healthy outlets like travel, hobbies, family, or faith—things they can openly share with others. Then, to keep the relationship from becoming one-sided, they repay the sources for the support. For instance, a hospital director I once worked with would compliment the cafeteria staff, calling them "the wonderful people who keep me fed!" He acknowledged his dependence on the cafeteria staff and expressed his gratitude and respect in return. Healthy dependence is not one-sided exploitation; it involves giving back and maintaining a balance.

By understanding and adopting healthy dependence, we can foster healthier relationships and personal growth. Recognizing our reliance on others and managing it maturely lead to a more balanced and fulfilling life.

Dependence May Trigger Narcissism

Relationships can't be formed in isolation. They require at least two entities, and both parties influence each other. It's hard to imagine that two people are in a genuine relationship if they don't have any influence on each other in any way. A characteristic in one person, be it emotional or behavioral, inevitably impacts the other, and even subconscious thoughts can be communicated. For example, when a parent is angry, the child feels frightened. When a boss smiles, employees feel at ease.

What then happens when someone reaches out to you for help? You naturally feel inclined to help. When we hear supplications like "We desperately need your help. Only you can help us," we feel inspired to assist despite our own hardships, perhaps by saving what little we have to make regular donations. Some of us go the opposite route; when we are out of resources, we decline requests for help and avoid those in need.

Psychiatrists explain that narcissism is awakened in those who are called upon to help. When the urge to let someone depend on us becomes overwhelming, we may develop an inflated view of our ability and value. Conversely, we might develop a defensive need to protect our remaining resources. Both reactions, though opposites, stem from a narcissistic inclination.

The Issue of Reward

When one person becomes dependent, the other may become a narcissist. A symbiotic relationship develops when one person feels valued and helps the other. The dependency and narcissism create an affectionate state of mutual need. Perhaps all love in the world starts out this way. When a mother holds her child for the first time, she feels an immense responsibility and aspires to be a perfect mother, wanting to provide perfect happiness to her child. This forms a strong bond of attachment.

Companies exploit this phenomenon. New employee orientations are essentially programs to awaken narcissism. In these, the company conveys how desperately they need the devotion of the new recruits. An experienced boss doesn't berate or rush the employee; instead, they humbly say, "I'm counting on you." This makes the employee determined to use all the abilities at their disposal to help the company and the boss.

For the relationship between dependency and narcissism to be maintained appropriately, adequate rewards are necessary. When employees provide labor, the employer must offer sufficient compensation to ensure employees can rely on them. Both parties need to satisfy dependency and self-love for the relationship to last. Even a dedicated mother can get exhausted from raising a child, but the child's growth provides joy as a reward. External validation from others—"You're doing a great job! Your kid is healthy and happy thanks to you!"—also helps maintain a healthy mother–child relationship.

However, problems arise when the balance of dependency and self-satisfaction is disrupted. If one side becomes excessively dependent, no amount of care will yield positive rewards, leading to exhaustion. The previously stimulated narcissism grows cold and turns into resentment.

Consequently, overly dependent individuals are eventually rejected, often getting hurt by the narcissistic person they relied on. Despite this, they tend to cling even more because unlike themselves, they see the other person as confident and healthy. Yet the narcissistic traits in the other person were nurtured by their own dependency. They get hurt by the exhausted narcissist's rejection and parting, unaware that it was the dependency that both nurtured the narcissist's confidence and drove them away.

Breaking Free from Excessive Dependency

Overly dependent people often hold three major misguided beliefs that leave them vulnerable to manipulation, harsh rejections, and a life of self-pity. The three misconceptions are as follows:

One, being alone is painful. This belief instills an excessive fear of not having a partner, family, or social group. Being alone does not make us ill, nor does it always mean we are being bullied, but the overly dependent see solitude as a sign of personal failure.

Two, someone will come along and save me. These individuals see themselves as uniquely inferior. They believe that others are whole and thus capable of helping them. "I envy ordinary people" is something such people often say. They come to rely on others in even worse situations, resulting in disappointment.

Three, being dependent is bad. People who believe this feel intense self-reproach if someone points out that they are dependent on others. Everyone leans on everyone else to some degree; what matters is how we depend on others and on whom we depend. Viewing dependency as inherently bad can result in a person's avoiding medical help, social life, or religious activities. Such people fail to recognize their dependency, continuing to be drawn to narcissists or turning ordinary people into narcissists, thereby inviting more pain and disappointment.

If you read this and find yourself wondering if you are overly dependent or tend to form immature dependence, that's perfectly fine. Acknowledging and recognizing the problem is a significant step. This self-awareness will help you gradually form mature, healthier dependence. If you feel you are already practicing healthy dependency, that's also good. Being content with yourself is a crucial process, indicating a growing sense of self-esteem.

Today's Exercise for Healthy Self-Esteem: What Should I Rely On?

First, let's acknowledge that the instinct to rely on something is natural for everyone. It's perfectly normal to want to fulfill this need.

Now consider what you should rely on. The object of your dependency should be stronger, healthier, and more wholesome than you. Relying on harmful substances like alcohol or tobacco will damage your body, while depending on gambling or infidelity can lead to personal ruin.

If you've been relying on smoking to cope with stress, it's time to find a new outlet for stress relief. Decide whether you'll turn to meditation when you're irritated and frustrated or call a partner to vent.

When choosing someone to rely on, find out if this person is trustworthy. Alternatively, relying on an abstract or deceased figure can be a good option. Personally, I draw strength and support from the memory of those who have already passed. While we can't know for sure about the afterlife, it's comforting to think that the deceased will always be there for me.

PART 3 CONCLUSION

The Protective Power of Healthy Distance

I recently came across a report stating that 80 percent of people who want to quit their jobs cite "interpersonal conflict" as the primary reason. Interpersonal issues are a persistent challenge for many, not only at work but also between friends, spouses, parents, children, and in-laws.

For those who struggle with interpersonal issues, I want to emphasize the importance of first and foremost maintaining a healthy distance. Let go of the desire to be close to everyone or to earn everyone's approval. Focus on surrounding yourself with people who get along with you, and don't invest your energy in those who do not.

Second, I want to highlight the principle of action and reaction. When you push others away, you are also pushed away. When you attack someone, your own heart suffers in equal measure. The more you hurt others, the more damage accumulates within you. This pain often circles back to you through different people and over time, making it hard to recognize that the original source of it was you.

Last, it's important to acknowledge that even the best

relationships have limits. There is no such thing as a perfect relationship. Even parent–child bonds can weaken, and siblings may see each other only once or twice a year. It's natural to grow distant from the family that raised you. So why exhaust yourself trying to maintain flawless relationships with people you meet in your social or professional life?

Many people torment themselves with obsessive thoughts about human relationships. Most employees already find it challenging to keep up with work demands, yet they spend immense energy managing workplace relationships. Instead of constantly pressuring yourself to get along with everyone at work, use that time to recharge. Just as you should forget about work once you clock out, try to let go of thoughts about your coworkers as well.

Self-Esteem Class Summary

- Much like self-respect, self-worth does not require external validation.
- Seek your own approval. Attempting to please others will only increase your stress and anxiety levels, working against the healthy development of your self-esteem.
- The work environment is not a good place to judge the health of your self-esteem. It is important to distinguish between your job, your career, and your dreams.
- We all have an innate desire to be needed and valued in society, but failing to feel validated in

one area doesn't mean you have to feel unwanted in all areas of life.

- Good decision-making has three key components: timeliness, knowing the scope of the decision, and knowing that there is no perfect decision.
- Decision-making blends both emotion and reason in equal measure.
- When it comes to negative past events, focus on setting goals by imagining alternative futures. Ask yourself, *What if?*
- It's human nature to be selfish. Embrace selfish altruism.
- There are three main types of unhealthy dependence: overdependence, misplaced dependence, and denial of one's dependence.

PART 4

Emotions That Get in the Way of Building Strong Self-Esteem

CHAPTER 18

Why Are Emotions So Hard to Control?

In this chapter, we'll explore the various emotions we experience in our daily lives. Emotions and self-esteem are deeply interconnected. Most of life's challenges are tied to emotions, and how we express and manage these emotions can change our lives. Despite its tremendous importance, surprisingly few people know how to express and control their emotions effectively.

When I ask clients during therapy what they felt in certain situations, rarely do I get a clear identification of their feelings. More than half deny they felt anything at all, avoid the question, or change the subject entirely. Initially, I was quite taken aback by such reactions. Why do people struggle to be honest about their emotions?

It didn't take me long to realize that this reaction is actually quite natural. Emotions belong to the realm of instincts, while verbal expression belongs to the realm of reason. Therefore, it's challenging for someone deeply enmeshed in an emotion to verbalize it accurately. Asking someone caught in their instincts to provide a rational explanation is like asking them to solve an impossible puzzle. Just as the phrase *at a loss for words* suggests, when emotions are intense, it's hard to speak at all. Only after some emotional distance is regained can we begin to reflect on our feelings.

Emotions: The Outfit of the Mind

Emotions are like the clothes our mind wears, revealing our inner state to the outside world. Thus the ability to regulate emotions is akin to having a good sense of fashion. Wearing well-made, stylish clothes can make you feel confident, while wearing rags can make you feel ashamed and self-conscious. However, just as the idea of perfect fashion is subjective, there are no absolutely good or absolutely bad emotions. Someone might wear the rough fabric of anger, sadness, or self-pity with vintage charm, while the bright clothes of happiness and joy may feel awkward if those feelings were imposed by someone else.

The emotions that govern our actions largely determine the health of our self-esteem. In this sense, how we manage our emotions can drastically alter the course of our lives.

The Relationship Between Emotion Regulation and Self-Esteem

Today, expressing one's emotions honestly, even at the risk of criticism, is seen as a virtue. We are encouraged to have the courage to be disliked or proudly refuse to suffer fools. There is a growing belief that a person who does not hide their emotions is a healthy person.

But is this really true? While expressing emotions is undoubtedly important, it's not always healthy or beneficial to let them out without restraint. Emotions, like hunger or sleepiness, belong to the realm of instincts, often felt subconsciously before we even notice them. Yet, just as consistently eating junk food can lead to diabetes or high blood pressure, and too little sleep can cause health problems, the same principle applies to expressing our emotions. Moderation is key.

Problems arise when we want to express anger moderately but end up exploding, or when we can't express our emotions at all. When we fail to regulate our emotions, our sense of self-control, a crucial component of self-esteem, is diminished.

Why We Feel Depressed After an Emotional Outburst

Understanding the process of how emotions form and translate into actions can provide a useful starting point for emotion regulation. When emotions surge, the brain senses a threat. Adrenaline, the neurotransmitter for aggression, floods in, while dopamine, the neurotransmitter for activity, floods the instinctual centers. At the same time, the frontal lobe, responsible for reason, shuts down. In this state, the brain prioritizes survival over rational thought, awakening the deepest, most instinctual part of the brain (the limbic system). This brain signal is quickly relayed to the body: *Warning! We are furious! Prepare for battle!* The body responds with an increased heart rate and rapid breathing. The brain interprets these physical changes as further evidence of a crisis, sending more warning signals back to the body in a feedback loop.

Without an effective brake, this tension escalates until it peaks and explodes. This results in actions like shouting or throwing objects in the moment when adrenaline peaks and dopamine activity is at its maximum. After reaching this peak, the brain rapidly shifts into a depressive state as a recovery mechanism. The body and brain, after a period of overstimulation, enter a rest phase. The brain halts adrenaline production, leading to feelings of lethargy, incompetence, and self-reproach.

Parents feeling guilty after yelling at their children or spouses feeling remorse after harsh words follows this pattern. Human evolution has embedded a cycle of depression following excitement as a safety measure. This natural brake mechanism, triggered by the brain, is essential for human survival, ensuring that we don't stay in a constant state of high alert.

Three Types of People Who Struggle with Emotion Regulation

The human brain and body survive through balanced regulation. However, some individuals find it particularly challenging to manage their emotions. These people typically act out habitually, have unprocessed traumas, or repress their emotions.

Emotion regulation is difficult for those who have a habit of acting out. When their brains enter a state of excitement, their hands, feet, and vocal cords react. When emotions peak, the emotional center in the deepest part of the brain becomes hyperactive. The body tries to divert this hyperactivity to other areas. For instance, physical activity like taking a deep breath, shadowboxing, or shouting on a mountaintop can help stabilize the emotional center. The problem arises when the physical releases become extreme and turn into physical aggression inflicted on others or oneself.

Unprocessed traumas also hinder emotion regulation. The hippocampus, the brain's memory center where past experiences are stored, is closely connected to the emotional center of the brain known as the amygdala. Therefore, for those with unresolved past traumas, the emotions associated with these memories remain raw and easily triggered. This heightened sensitivity can lead to frequent anxiety, especially if the past trauma is associated with extreme fear. The triggering manifests in much the same way as people taking out their unprocessed anger on the wrong people.

Repressing emotions is also a failure to regulate emotions. Some people rarely show anger, hatred, or sadness because they view experiencing emotions as a sign of weakness. They don't lack feelings; they simply reject them. New mothers who believe they must be patient with their child at all times, new employees who think they must keep their heads down and work without complaint, and students who feel they must focus solely on studying often repress their emotions. Their natural emotional responses evoke guilt. Like a person on a diet trying to ignore hunger, this behavior is essentially a denial of their human instincts.

Characteristics of People Who Manage Emotions Well

People who struggle with emotion regulation often oscillate between repression and explosion. When angry with a partner, they might resort to passive-aggression: "I'm not angry. But just out of curiosity, why are you late?" They suppress their emotions despite physical signs like an increased heart rate and tears. The pressure builds until they explode, harming themselves and others.

In contrast, those who manage emotions well are aware of what they are feeling, how strong the feeling is, and how it is affecting them. They understand that their anger toward a subordinate, for example, stems not just from the immediate situation but also from past experiences and how stressed or tired they are today. These individuals avoid making important decisions or commitments while emotionally charged, waiting for the emotional wave to pass before acting. It might seem as though they are suppressing their emotions, but in reality, they are choosing not to act impulsively. Instead of shouting, they might take a deep breath, leave the room, or fix their hair and clothes. Everyone experiences intense emotions; the difference lies in how discreetly one manages them. Some wait for the feelings to subside while others unleash them for all to see.

Today's Exercise for Healthy Self-Esteem: The Emotion Journal

To regulate our feelings, we must first acknowledge them. Emotions are like waves in front of us. Rather than being swept away, we should prepare to ride these waves. For those who have long been overwhelmed by their emotions, even looking at the waves can be daunting. But to ride the wave, you must first look at it. Therefore, practicing awareness is the first step.

Recall all the events of your day from morning to night, and jot down the emotions you felt at each moment. This will reveal what your recurring emotions are. If a particular emotion appears more than three times, note the related events or thoughts. This exercise is called the emotion journal. The key to an emotion journal is the conclusion: Always end with a reflection or observation rather than a question. Finishing with "Why did I feel this way?" can intensify the emotion and cause self-blame or depression.

For example:

My manager scolded me. I felt misunderstood and angry.

My husband got annoyed because the house was a mess. I felt hurt.

When I lay down to sleep, tears suddenly flowed. My life is pitiful. I felt sorry for myself.

Conclusion: Why does everything get me down? This has been a tough day!

CHAPTER 19

Things to Discern for Emotion Regulation

Self-esteem is a measure of how much we respect ourselves, but self-esteem is also considered a type of emotion. This is why it is crucial for us to have healthy self-esteem in order to distinguish and handle the various emotions we experience. Some understanding of psychology can be helpful in this regard. Emotions are like electricity—they are essential for daily life, but mishandling them can lead to shocks.

Emotions Come with Labels

Regulating emotions is akin to driving a car. Even if you have a fancy car, it's useless if you can't drive it or if the car doesn't respond to your commands. You need the skill to stop where you want to stop and move in the direction you desire. Once you've mastered the basics of driving, you also need to know the finer details—which pedal increases the car's speed or which button adjusts the interior temperature.

The same applies to emotions. To have mastery over

your emotions, you must know which emotions you're feeling—their characteristics and the similarities and differences between them. Fortunately, humans have come up with names for many of the emotions we experience.

Naming emotions is important because word retrieval is a cognitive skill. An interesting study published in a neurosurgery journal in February 2009 found that many patients who underwent brain surgery due to tumors or accidents struggled to recall names when seeing people or objects. Further analysis revealed that this difficulty was more prominent in patients with damage to the left frontal and anterior temporal lobes. In particular, the ability to put names to faces was significantly impaired in patients with frontal lobe damage.

When emotions intensify, the brain's focus shifts to the limbic system or the limbic circuit. Brain activity is concentrated in this area, resulting in hardly any function in the cortical areas, like the frontal lobe. To release the brain from this emotion-focused state, one must find a way to regain balance in brain activity so that the other parts of the brain can function properly again.

Using emotion cards is an effective tool for calming emotions. I often show emotion cards to clients, providing them with an opportunity to rationally grasp what emotions they're experiencing.

Five Steps for Calming Emotions

During my psychiatry residency, I encountered cognitive behavioral therapy (CBT) theory at a workshop. CBT begins by categorizing all situations and experiences into a few distinct groups, like elements on the periodic table. From a CBT perspective, the world is divided into events, thoughts, emotions, and actions.

Given my fondness for categorization, I found CBT particularly appealing. What's more astonishing is that as I began sorting events and my reactions to them into these categories, my entire life started to change noticeably. For example, I lose sleep when my emotions fluctuate. One night, as I lay awake fretting, I thought of CBT and decided to apply it.

I can't sleep at night. What emotion triggered this action? Upon reflection, I realized my heart was pounding and I was experiencing shortness of breath as well. It was anxiety. Delving deeper into why I felt anxious, I found myself consumed by the thought *Can I be a good father?* So what was the event that triggered this thought? My wife told me she was pregnant a few days ago. An event led to a thought, which led to an emotion, which led to a physical response.

Situation: *My wife is pregnant.*
Thought: *Will I make a good father?*
Emotion: *Anxiety, fear*
Physical response: *Insomnia, heart palpitation*

Action: *I sit alone at night staring off into space.*
Solution: *Tomorrow morning, I'll do research on how to be a good father.*

Thus, by organizing events, thoughts, emotions, actions, and now even physical responses, I was able to regain some peace of mind.

Categorization is an act of rational thinking. If brain activity is moved from the realm of emotions to the realm of reason, emotions can be managed, allowing one the clarity to identify problems and devise solutions.

However, this method does not always work. When one has suffered severe trauma or when pathological conditions persist, overall cognitive abilities decline, including the ability to discern what we are feeling.

In such cases, everything gets tangled up. The limbic system and memory centers become disorganized. Only memories associated with sadness or anger come to mind when we are overwhelmed with sadness and anger, and this flood of negative memories leads to an even greater surge of negative emotions. Moreover, stress blurs the lines between past, present, and future. One's own emotions can become confused with the emotions of others as well. Past traumas turn into worries about the future—*What if the same thing happens again?*—and *I'm worthless* turns into *Others also think I'm pathetic.*

This vicious cycle, which occurs between one's inner emotions and memories, has a way of expanding across time and space to include the past, future, and external world. Therefore, when emotion regulation falters, it's essential to clearly identify where the emotions are coming from. One must strive to tell the difference between past emotions, current feelings and future expectations. Moreover, it's crucial to confirm that all of these are just emotions one is experiencing.

Managing Emotions in Challenging Situations

It's rare to find someone who is naturally adept at identifying and categorizing their emotions from the start. In fact, if someone were to preemptively categorize their emotions before truly feeling them, one might be viewed as obsessive. However, it's clear that once you immerse yourself in an emotion and then follow the steps to process it, you can almost always find your way out of that emotional state.

Yet there are times when managing emotions is exceptionally hard despite our best efforts. This often occurs when our brain functions are disrupted either socially or biologically. For example, after prolonged sleep deprivation or when in love, our physical and emotional states are far from normal. Many people mistakenly believe that failure to manage emotions under these vulnerable circumstances is a sign of weakness, but such misconception can lead to self-loathing. Here are some scenarios that present an extra challenge to emotion regulation:

When Dealing with Family Matters

Emotions tied to family can be particularly challenging because we often confuse our family's feelings with our own. We might feel deeply involved in the emotions of our family members or mistakenly believe they share our exact feelings. For instance, if a family member is ill, we suffer more than we would if a person not related to us was sick. If our parents are insulted, we get angrier than if it happened to a stranger. As the emotional weight related to family grows, managing it becomes tougher.

When Under the Influence of Alcohol

Alcohol shifts brain function to the limbic system, which governs instincts, thus weakening the prefrontal cortex responsible for reason and motor function. This can lead to confusing past memories with current emotions and blurring the lines between oneself and others, often resulting in conflicts.

When You Are Hungry or Sleep-Deprived

In these states, the body goes into crisis mode. The thalamus, a deep brain structure, oversees diet and sleep. Prolonged lack of sleep or glucose can trigger a state of emergency in the thalamus, impairing reason and leaving only survival instincts. This can lead to excessive aggression or binge-eating.

When You Are in Love

Similar to being under the influence of alcohol or in a family-related scenario, reason is paralyzed when one is in love. Especially in love, the use of excessive suppression mechanisms arises from the belief that negative emotions should be avoided. Many mothers, for instance, struggle with emotion regulation despite loving their children intensely, simply because the depth of their love makes emotion regulation harder.

When Situations Hit Too Close to Home

Sympathy and pity are powerful motivators that lead to action. This is why we simply can't ignore the plight of close friends or colleagues experiencing situations similar to our own dilemmas.

When faced with these scenarios, it is best to first acknowledge that managing your emotions might be challenging. Don't believe you can control your emotions 100 percent. Accepting that even partial control is a success is crucial. Overfocusing on emotion regulation in these situations can lead to self-loathing or feelings of guilt, depleting the energy needed to manage emotions effectively.

Today's Exercise for Healthy Self-Esteem: Distinguishing Thoughts, Actions, and Emotions

Recall an emotion or incident you experienced today and answer the questions.

For example:

Event: *I was criticized by my boss for a minor mistake today.*

What do you feel when you think about this incident?
Frustration. Embarrassment.

What do you feel about yourself when you think of this incident?
I'm useless. I might get fired.

What physical reactions do you experience from head to toe when you think of this incident?
My heart races and my face feels hot.

What actions did you take as a result of this incident? How would you like to react in the future?
I ended up binge-eating. In the future, I want to talk it out over coffee with a friend instead.

CHAPTER 20

Managing Difficult Emotions— Embarrassment, Emptiness, and Ambivalence

A successful comedian once announced his sudden retirement. One day, while putting on makeup, he was struck by a sense of embarrassment. He wondered, *What if my kids see this?* and *How long can I keep doing this?* He went up on the stage that day and found himself unable to commit to his role. As an embarrassed comedian, he could no longer make people laugh. No matter how popular or wealthy he was, enduring daily embarrassment was unbearable. Eventually, he retired and started a business.

Embarrassment is like a beehive in the heart. If you disturb it, hidden anger, inferiority, and wounds burst out. Handle it gently, and you might get sweet honey, but it's best to stay away if you cannot keep it under control.

Even seasoned performers struggle to manage their emotions when faced with embarrassment on the stage. Feeling ashamed or humiliated can be troubling for anyone. While some might be able to maneuver past it with greater ease, few remain unaffected by embarrassment.

Common Misconceptions
About Embarrassment

Embarrassment often stems from worrying about how others perceive us. This emotion is a product of being a social animal. Many young people boldly claim, "Who cares what others think?" but are just as influenced by internet comments and social media.

Several misconceptions cause frequent embarrassment. First, we mistakenly believe that everyone is watching us. Think of a group photo—it's easy to understand. You might feel upset because you're the only one in the group photo who closed their eyes or is making a strange face. However, just as you care about your appearance, others care about their own. Most people don't notice what you're wearing, if your makeup is smudged, or if your eyes are closed.

Second, we tend to be too critical of ourselves. Most of us judge ourselves pretty harshly. We believe that there has to be a valid reason behind everything we do. In reality, others don't pay much attention to what we do or how our behaviors change, and if they do notice our mistakes, they very seldom judge us as harshly as we judge ourselves.

Last, we think that others will remember our embarrassing moment long into the future. Suppose you find out that colleagues or friends are gossiping behind your back. The shock, humiliation, and sense of betrayal can be overwhelming. However, this is a misconception. For them, gossip is just light conversation. People aren't interested enough in others to fixate on their mistakes.

Emptiness: The Emotional Vacuum

Embarrassment is a dense emotion, entangled with thoughts about others' judgments, and their intensity and duration. On the opposite end of the spectrum is emptiness. Feeling nothing—neither excitement nor shame—is what we call numbness or emptiness.

Emptiness itself isn't a negative emotion. Many strive to clear their minds of thoughts and emotions. Just as inactivity is seen as rest, emotionally exhausted people often say, "I just want to think about nothing at all." Thus emptiness is the feeling that follows when we clear our heads.

However, many find emptiness distressing. Despite wanting to forget everything due to deep psychological burdens, reaching this desired state often feels futile. Why? Because people don't realize that emptiness was what they sought. They set goals for earning money or achieving success but rarely define emotional goals. They hope to feel "something better than this," not knowing what that means. Therefore, even when they subconsciously desire emptiness, they fail to recognize it when they do achieve it.

This can lead to rejecting or developing a negative perception of emptiness, resulting in harmful actions. Emptiness is an emotional vacuum, and in an attempt to fill this void, people might hastily engage in activities like starting a new relationship. Although it temporarily masks emptiness, it can lead to unwanted relationships and further dissatisfaction.

When repeated, this process creates a mental association

between emptiness and negative actions, equating emptiness with painful experiences. Consequently, attempts to erase emptiness usually end in regret, making people perceive emptiness as a negative emotion.

Ambivalence: Loving and Hating Simultaneously

We sometimes experience alternating conflicting emotions. This is known as ambivalence. This includes feelings of love and hate, or the urge to eat despite not wanting to.

Ambivalence often emerges when discussing relationship issues. If a friend asks for advice about breaking up and you suggest ending the relationship, they might suddenly argue, "How can I? I'll never find someone like this again." Conversely, if you advise staying together, they might continue to complain about the difficulties. This cycle of conflicting emotions is common in love stories.

Those who are exceptionally susceptible to ambivalence have a way of draining the mental energy from those around them as well. When friends take them out to dinner and offer them heartfelt advice, the ambivalent person does not heed the advice. If things turn out well, the ambivalent person does not bother to say thank you, as they've exhausted their mental energy being pulled in opposite directions; they have no energy left to spend on those around them.

Recognizing Your Core Emotions

So far we've explored three challenging emotions: embarrassment, emptiness, ambivalence. If you're struggling with emotion regulation, it's likely that one of these emotions is frequently surfacing.

Everyone has emotions that they experience more intensely than others, known as core emotions. For instance, those who often feel embarrassment are particularly sensitive to others' opinions, perceiving mere glances as ridicule. Someone whose core emotion is feeling belittled may frequently experience self-deprecation and resentment. They might harbor hostility toward others even before recognizing their own feelings.

Identifying your core emotion is the first step to managing it. Core emotions vary from person to person and can include feelings like resentment, anger, or shame. You might have more than one core emotion.

The solutions to these emotions also vary. For some, simply recognizing the emotion can bring relief, while others might need different strategies. The key is that mastering one core emotion can help in managing others. In the following chapters, we will classify emotions by intensity and explore how to regulate them.

Today's Exercise for Healthy Self-Esteem: Reflect on Your Core Emotions

Identifying your core emotions is crucial. Recognizing when they surface helps you acknowledge, *Ah, my core emotion of* [insert your core emotion here] *is acting up again today!* Acknowledging your emotions is vital because failure to do so can lead to self-criticism, like, *What's wrong with me?* Instead, simply make the observation that your core emotion is surfacing. Asking *why* can lead to self-reproach, but observing without judgment allows you to process your emotions.

People with low self-esteem often waste energy questioning their core emotions. They ask, *Is my core emotion really embarrassment? What if it's something else?* Remember, you can have multiple core emotions that can change daily or remain undefined. Like childhood dreams, core emotions can evolve, and it's not a problem if they do.

Do not stress about pinpointing your core emotion. Instead, simply reflect on it. Just asking yourself what your core emotion is can contribute to a healthier mind.

CHAPTER 21

Managing "Hot" Emotions— Self-Loathing, Guilt, Self-Pity, and Self-Love

Emotions are like the weather—there are bound to be both rainy and sunny days. Similarly, emotional changes are completely normal. A weather forecaster doesn't control the weather but understands it enough to advise using sunscreen on sunny days and umbrellas on rainy days. Similarly, those who manage their emotions well do not aim to eliminate or change them but to understand and respond appropriately.

However, those with low self-esteem are often dissatisfied with their emotions. This is akin to complaining about the strong sun on sunny days or the humidity on rainy days. Weather changes are beyond human control; we can only adapt to them as they occur.

The reason for constantly discussing emotions in self-esteem management is precisely this. To cope with emotions, we must first understand them. We need to recognize whether it is snowing or raining and grasp the characteristics of these emotions.

The Four Spectrums of Intense Emotions

Many people grow up being taught to suppress emotions. From a young age, they hear phrases like "Don't cry" or "Boys shouldn't whine," internalizing the need to hide sadness and anguish. Nowadays, there's a counterreaction that emphasizes the power of positivity, which can create an obsession with dismissing negative emotions. How can we learn to accept and express our natural emotions in such a context?

To be happy, our emotional receptors must be active, healthy, and capable of handling all emotions. Positive and negative emotions come hand in hand. If we fear negative emotions, our brain starts to dull overall emotional perception, hardening all emotional receptors to avoid bad feelings. Frequent emotional changes can be problematic due to sensitivity, while fear of emotions leads to insensitivity.

There are intense emotions categorized as "hot" emotions. These aren't inherently bad, but it is advisable to keep an appropriate distance from them. The terms for the emotions vary slightly, depending on whether they are directed outwardly or toward oneself.

Anger vs. Self-Loathing

Anger is a fiery emotion. Holding on to anger is like holding a burning coal. Because it burns at the slightest touch, people often try to avoid it. Holding on to it for too long harms not only the mind but also the body.

Like flames, anger quickly engulfs us. When we meet an angry person, we often try to avoid them or attempt to extinguish their anger. Sometimes people respond with even greater anger to quell the other's fury, the logic being that we should fight fire with fire. If skilled at managing this, one might be able to control the other's anger, but failure results in doubling the damage.

Those who frequently feel anger often harbor self-loathing. They get angry at themselves when alone and at their family when with them, hurting their nearest and dearest with their inner self-hatred.

If you often find yourself angry, carefully examine its intensity and direction. Focusing too much on the target of your anger can make you forget about your self-loathing. Reflecting on questions like, *When was the last time I was not angry about something?* and *Is this truly something to be angry about or do I just have a lot of anger inside?* is the first step to managing anger.

Hatred vs. Guilt

Hatred is not as intense as anger but is still a dangerous emotion. Holding it too close or for too long causes low-grade burns. It's like very spicy food—okay in moderation, but too much can cause stomach problems.

We cannot go through life avoiding everyone we dislike. Even family members, sometimes even children, can evoke feelings of hatred. So feeling hatred toward others is natural. When we suppress hatred, we may end up repressing emotions altogether or resort to immature defense mechanisms. This includes compulsions like the "good child" syndrome, in which you feel compelled to be kind to everyone and constantly do good deeds.

Living with self-directed hatred, or guilt, is also an immature defense mechanism. Fear of external criticism leads to preemptive self-blame as a protective measure. For instance, if your child is struggling, you might say to them, "I have failed you as a parent." Such self-reproach not only fails to console the child but also makes them defensive. Self-directed aggression is still aggression, and a contagious one at that. This guilt is likely to transfer to the child.

Pity vs. Self-Pity

Pity is a feeling of sympathy for others. Unlike anger and hatred, this is a compassionate emotion. We were taught from a young age that this is a good sentiment, but this isn't always the case.

When we offer pity to someone who isn't ready to receive it, we can cause conflict. Some would prefer to appear confident and be the object of envy. If there is something lacking in their lives or there are areas they need help with, they'd prefer to suffer quietly than ask for help. They believe that keeping their needs hidden is the way to protect their pride. When we offer our pity to these people, we end up hurting their feelings.

On the other hand, feeling pity and sympathy for yourself is called self-pity. When we refer to self-pity, it is mostly used in a negative sense. It involves thinking of yourself as pitiful, believing others are out to get you, or, in severe cases, seeing yourself as a victim. You may regard yourself as the victim of abusive parenting, the broken education system, toxic workplace dynamics, or a bad marriage.

People who are trapped in self-pity often evoke sympathy from others. This can help them easily make friends and receive assistance. However, it also makes it hard for them to escape their self-pity. For example, parents who feel sympathy for their children may delay their independence, or one might stay in a romantic relationship out of pity for one's partner.

Thus, couples in which one feels sympathy and the other feels self-pity often face limits in deepening their relationship. If one of them cannot overcome their self-pity despite their partner's best efforts, it eventually hurts the partner's feelings. A person stuck in a self-pitying state, meanwhile, is afraid to move on from the state of self-pity for fear that the attention and sympathy the partner offers will stop.

Attraction, Self-Love, and Attention

Feeling attracted to someone means taking an interest in that person. Our brain is naturally wired to enjoy and seek out focus and concentration. There are many contesting arguments about what is good or bad for the brain, but what the brain truly desires is to have an object of attention and focus.

Love, in essence, is the brain finding something or someone to focus on. Attraction is a milder psychological response compared to love. When you feel attracted to someone, you become curious about their lives, thoughts, and more. Interest and attraction spark the beginning of love, and when love fades, attention is the first thing to disappear. When a partner cheats, the sense of betrayal stems from the perception that they've focused their attention on someone else.

Self-love means having an interest in yourself. When we love ourselves, we tend to pay attention to what we like, what we want, and so on. When this self-interest becomes excessive, it turns into narcissism—an exclusive focus on what pleases oneself, a form of selfish love.

Life would be simpler if we could only like the right people and show interest in those who interest us. But life is messy, and sometimes we end up feeling affection for those we shouldn't. Cheating is one such example. Cheating literally means to act unfairly or dishonestly. In other words, it is unfair and dishonest to all involved. In such situations, the best course of action is to withdraw those feelings. However, emotions don't always adhere to reason. This is when efforts to redirect your focus can help. Keeping a distance, both physically and mentally, helps distract the brain from the source of those feelings, allowing the emotions to fade.

Conversely, it can be challenging when you cannot stop resenting someone you ought to love, such as a child or spouse. Likewise, you may find yourself filled with self-loathing and anger despite efforts to love yourself. In such cases, managing emotions through interest and focus is essential. Even if the feeling of love for your spouse isn't constant, showing interest in various aspects of their life is crucial. Simple gestures of interest such as asking, "Did you eat?" or "What are you doing now?" allocate a portion of your attention to them. Dedicating even 30 percent of your total headspace to your spouse can improve the relationship. While this won't instantly revive love, it will help maintain a peaceful relationship compared to being consumed by hatred or anger.

The same principle applies when dealing with self-dissatisfaction. Instead of trying to fall in love with yourself overnight, take little steps. Pay continuous attention to your thoughts, likes, and dislikes, including what makes you anxious, what makes you happy, and what kind of gifts you'd like to receive.

Today's Exercise for Healthy Self-Esteem: Pay Attention to Yourself

People with low self-esteem often focus too much on others, being overly conscious of others' opinions and thoughts. This focus detracts from the attention they should be giving to themselves. To shift focus to yourself, start by paying attention to yourself. Writing an autobiography or regularly checking in on your current state can be helpful. Knowing yourself better than anyone is crucial.

For instance:

Where were you born?

Who are your family members?

What is your relationship with your family like?

What were your school days like?

What is your current lifestyle like?

What are the things that make you feel good or bad?

Who are the people you like and what are their characteristics?

What are your strengths and weaknesses?

What are your dreams? (Or what were your dreams if you have none now?)

What type of person do you aspire to be?

CHAPTER 22

Managing "Cold" Emotions— Disappointment, Neglect, Cynicism, Indifference

Everyone has emotions they enjoy and emotions they find difficult to endure. Depending on one's profession or situation, certain emotions are more necessary than others. For example, doctors are often associated with coolheadedness, while artists are associated with passion. A doctor must not be overly emotional or passionate when treating patients, as this could lead to serious mistakes.

Some of us are more cynical or cold than most. While cold emotions can feel negative compared to warm emotions, they are necessary. There are no right or wrong emotions, but it's essential to manage them well when they become overwhelming.

Types of Cold Emotions

People whose emotions often run cold have developed this strategy for a reason. There are certainly some benefits to choosing cold emotions rather than hot ones. However, just as staying out in the cold for too long can lead to issues like catching a cold or experiencing frostbite, it is important to guard against becoming too cold and repressing feelings.

There was a time when I tried to be coldhearted. Around the start of my adolescence, I thought, *I'm too sentimental. From now on, I'll live coldheartedly*, believing I wasn't tough enough. For twenty years, my resolve hardly changed. I still feel easily shaken, cry often, and blush easily. Yet at some point, people began to tell me I seemed cold. Some cried because of my harsh words and others found me too cynical to be around. Realizing this, I practiced smiling in front of a mirror and read poetry to soften myself. Despite these efforts, my stern expression and cynical tone became part of my personality. I now regret striving to be so cold. There's nothing wrong with shedding tears or being affectionate. I succeeded in becoming cold, but my judgment back then was flawed.

There are times in life when you need to be cold, and cold emotions aren't always bad. However, excessive coldness leads to problems. If you frequently experience cooling or numbing emotions, consider which of these core emotions are at play. Observe closely to understand where you stand.

Disappointment vs. Sadness and Depression

When you say you're disappointed, it means you had expectations that were let down. You expected a delicious meal that wasn't there, thought you were loved but weren't, or expected hot water but got cold instead. In other words, disappointment is the emotion that arises when expectations aren't met.

Some people are always ready to be disappointed, regardless of how much they have or enjoy. They tend to set expectations unrealistically high or anticipate disappointment. Even when something good happens, they tell themselves that it was just a fluke or a stroke of good luck.

There are also those who often disappoint others. While some do this maliciously, many do so with good intentions. They regularly cause little disappointments so that others will not have high expectations of them. For example, a partner may show disappointing traits early to prepare for when the rose-tinted glasses eventually come off, or a boss may point out all the details a client might take issue with instead of praising an employee for completing a big project. These people sprinkle disappointment to manage expectations or keep a subordinate hungry for approval.

When disappointment is repeated, it turns into sadness. Disappointment settles into the heart. So to avoid sadness, one lowers one's expectations or avoids thinking about the future. High recurrence of sadness can lead to depression. You become lethargic, lose motivation, and feel drained. However, not many people recognize or admit to feeling depressed. This might be because they fear being labeled with the illness of depression.

Disregard vs. Pessimism

To disregard someone can mean to underestimate them or to neglect them. Underestimating others involves belittling and looking down on them, which is more a thought than an emotion. However, many people explode with emotion when they feel underestimated. Thus placing underestimation in the category of an emotion seems fitting. Feeling ignored evokes aggressive emotions. The second type, overlooking, falls under indifference—a cold emotion.

Both types of ignoring are harmful when directed at oneself. Self-esteem drops easily when you are belittled or neglected. It's natural that you can't respect yourself if others look down on or ignore you. Prolonged neglect of yourself leads to negative emotions, making you view everything related to yourself pessimistically. Ultimately, being belittled or overlooked causes you to see the world negatively.

Cynicism vs. Apathy

In today's world, cynicism seems to be on the rise. Cynical people often show no expression or exhibit a cold "so what?" attitude. Is cynicism a bad or a good emotion?

I was somewhat older than my peers when I served in the military. I recall something a platoon leader said during training: "When something annoys you, just laugh it off." Confused by the regimented life, I tried following his advice. Whenever I got angry, I laughed. Whether it was a drill instructor's yelling, washing dishes, or the water cutting off during a shower, I forced a smile. It was more of a grimace, but it surprisingly helped cool my emotions.

I realized that this forced smile was a form of cynicism. Cold yet not overtly aggressive, cynicism helps manage emotions without attacking anyone. However, prolonged cynicism can lead to apathy—a lack of joy or sadness. Cynically cool people often experience this. They avoid stress but also miss out on happiness, leading to all-round apathy. The brain loves focus, but with cold emotions, the heart loses its focus, leading to the emptiness of apathy. Therefore, cynical people should engage in hobbies or relationships to prevent their emotional temperature from dipping below a certain level.

Indifference vs. Lethargy

Indifference is the most intense of the cold emotions. For any feeling to arise, one needs to direct and focus attention on a person or an object. When we are experiencing indifference, we cannot offer even the smallest interest.

People used to tell me to mind my own business because I was overly sensitive and cared too much about other people. But I eventually learned to use indifference to my benefit. Despite remaining sensitive, I could withdraw my focus if needed. It was liberating; I no longer cared about things or people I disliked. How did I achieve this?

The key to change is to always want. I recognized and

repeatedly reminded myself that I *wanted* to be indifferent. I constantly told my brain that I didn't want to hate or seek revenge but to be indifferent. The brain then instructed me to look away and keep a distance. Failing that, I read novels to immerse myself in something else. This was my method of cultivating indifference.

Many want to disconnect from unwanted interests but fear indifference, worrying it might lead to lethargy or lack of volition. However, this is like worrying about hypothermia while treating a fever. Our brain has an automatic control system to maintain balance. It would take more than a temporary infusion of indifference during a moment of emotional intensity to become lethargic.

Today's Exercise for Healthy Self-Esteem: Find Actions That Control Emotional Temperature

In this chapter, we've categorized emotions by temperature. Properly managing emotions means knowing how to mix them appropriately. When you're bubbling over with anger, you need to add cold emotions, and when you're stuck in lethargy or cynicism, you need to warm up with hot emotions.

For example, when I read novels, I choose works that match my emotional state to maintain balance. Some authors' works give me energy and vitality, while others help me regain calmness. If nothing else works, I watch my favorite American sitcom, *Friends,* which never fails to lift my spirits.

Each of us has actions that either increase or reduce our emotional temperature. Meeting friends, watching TV, playing games, or shopping—all these activities are connected to our emotional temperature. Once you know what warms you up and what cools you down, it becomes much easier to manage your emotions.

For example:

Actions that heat up my emotions: *Watching movies and TV shows, running, being physically active.*

Actions that cool down my emotions: *Deep breathing, sleeping, doing Pilates, reminiscing about past relationships, thinking about past failures.*

PART 4 CONCLUSION

Harnessing Emotional Energy

Many people believe their emotions define them. However, you are not your emotions. Emotions are just energy you can use. Think of life as riding a bicycle. The emotions you experience determine your speed. Anger or anxiety speeds you up, while cynicism slows you down. But a bicycle's movement is not solely about speed; the direction you steer is even more crucial. This decision is made by reason. You might need to apply the brakes to control your speed, but you don't need to be overly concerned with how fast you are going. On uphill climbs, your speed will naturally decrease, and on downhill slopes, you should enjoy the speed. Emotions are important, but they're not everything. Recognizing what you feel and responding appropriately is the key.

Use this understanding to navigate your emotional landscape effectively, adjusting your actions to maintain balance and control in your life. This way, you can steer your journey with both reason and emotional intelligence, ensuring a smoother and more fulfilling ride.

Self-Esteem Class Summary

- Emotions belong to the realm of instincts, while verbal expression belongs to the realm of reason.
- When we fail to regulate our emotions, our sense of self-control, a crucial component of self-esteem, diminishes.
- To repress your emotions is to deny your human instincts.
- From a CBT perspective, the world is divided into events, thoughts, emotions, and actions (physical actions). Thus it becomes useful to organize events into these categories.
- Three challenging and recurring emotions are embarrassment, emptiness, and ambivalence. If you're struggling with emotion regulation, it's likely that one of these emotions is surfacing.
- Our brain is naturally wired to enjoy and seek out focus and concentration. Aim to turn that focus inward.

PART 5

Habits to Break
for Self-Esteem Recovery

CHAPTER 23

The Habit of Preemptive Defeat

Once, I was watching a national football match. Early in the game, the Korean team got a penalty kick opportunity, but it ended in failure. It wasn't that our player kicked poorly; the opposing goalkeeper made an excellent save. People started getting anxious.

A friend watching the game with me at the pub said, "We've lost. Why bother continue watching? We missed a penalty kick, so we're definitely going to lose!" And sure enough, we conceded the first goal. My friend's voice rose: "We missed the penalty, conceded the first goal, and now our main defender is injured. We're completely done for. We're going to lose 3-0 or 5-0." He then started drinking heavily.

I've noticed this friend has a habit of overreacting to bad situations. He tends to blow things out of proportion, making them seem worse than they are. It was entertaining to be around him when he was worked up, but I also felt bad for him. Why? Because after my friend gave up and turned in, our team finally got one point ahead. He slept through that exhilarating moment.

How to Avoid Being Devastated
by Disappointment

There are moments in life when we feel utterly ruined. Whether it's failing an exam or experiencing a breakup, we often say we've hit rock bottom. While it's true that disappointment can help us grow, it seems there are too many situations these days where we feel devastated.

Modern society exposes people to more stress than was the case in previous eras. In our information and industrialized society, we're subjected to far more pressures than people experience in agrarian societies. While older generations may think young people today are weak-willed, I do not agree. The more developed a civilization, the greater the stress.

A clear example is the multitude of exams we must pass. Entrance exams, job applications, promotions, and business qualifications. To start a business, you need approval from the tax office, the district office, the health department, and the bank. We're constantly under scrutiny and often face the prospect of failure.

I believe the real hardship comes from our yearning for affection. It's now widely accepted that parental love is crucial for a child's development. This has led many adults to look back on their upbringing and feel they didn't receive enough love from their parents and, in turn, to worry that they're not giving them enough attention and support.

Consequently, many people worry that they are suffering from emotional deprivation and self-diagnose attachment disorders. They believe their lack of parental love has damaged their ability to form healthy relationships. When conflicts arise, they might think, *I'm the only one who reacts this way* or *All my relationships are doomed.*

This habit of despair reduces our resilience to stress. We lose confidence before the inevitable stressors in life like breakups and big exams. When we lose focus and our hearts begin to race, we might think, *I'm unstable because I wasn't loved.* This declining confidence leads to a belief in inevitable failure.

We often despair because of anxiety about tests or relationships. However, some people manage to navigate these challenges despite the many potential triggers for despair. Stressors are everywhere, but we do have the choice of not engaging with them.

The Catalyst for Despair: Catastrophizing

Modern society is filled with triggers for despair. When these meet the "spark" of catastrophizing, despair and hopelessness quickly follow.

Catastrophizing is the thought that all hope is lost. A minor trigger can lead to thoughts of death, bankruptcy, or other tragedies, paralyzing rational thought. For example, before an interview, most of us feel nervous. We might think, *I'm a bit nervous, I should take a deep breath.* Some of us may need to pace the hall to calm down, while others may get through the interview just fine without doing a thing.

However, when someone catastrophizes, the problem

intensifies. They might think, *My heart is racing, I'm screwed.* This thought escalates to *I'll freeze up in the interview. I won't be able to get a word out. I'm going to fail,* and then to *My partner will leave me because I'm a failure. I'll be alone, and when my parents die, then I'll die alone.*

Normal levels of stress and anxiety can lead to a catastrophic response, causing someone to prematurely despair and give up. They might think they're despairing because they've failed, but in reality, they failed because they gave up.

Facing the End of Your Catastrophizing

Catastrophizing is like an allergy. Some people have no reaction to pollen, dust mites, or nuts, while others experience runny noses, hives, or even difficulty breathing. Knowing what triggers your allergies allows you to avoid those substances or take appropriate medication.

Similarly, to manage your catastrophizing reactions, you need to understand what your fears are. This isn't easy to discern in everyday life, so therapists often ask the same question repeatedly to get to the root of it. When a client is anxious about a potential outcome, they ask, "What do you think will happen next?" By repeating this question, they help clients uncover their core fear.

Once a man confided in me that he felt an overwhelming fear of death. A few hours earlier, he had received a call from a client indicating a payment delay. This wasn't unusual, and typically he would shrug it off. But on this particular day, his catastrophizing reaction kicked in, leading to extreme anxiety. I asked him, "So what do you think will happen next?"

"I think I won't be able to pay the interest," he replied.

"And then what will happen?"

"Other payments will also be delayed, and I won't be able to pay the interest consistently."

"And then?"

"Eventually I'll go bankrupt, and creditors will come after me."

"So what will happen after that?"

"My family will be ruined. They might all blame me and resent me."

"And then what do you think will happen?"

"Um . . . I guess I'll end up alone."

"And then?"

"I'll probably die alone and miserable."

When we reached this point, he seemed to relax. He realized that his anxiety was not about the immediate situation but about a distant, unlikely scenario.

Most of our despair stems from such thoughts. The real issue isn't the current situation but the fear that it will spiral into a catastrophe. Once you identify what you're actually worried about, you often find that the problem is manageable. Transforming vague, nebulous anxiety into specific, realistic concerns allows you to either find solutions for it or let it go.

The Four Major Fears: Death, Bankruptcy, Separation, and Loss of Attractiveness

People's fears generally fall into four categories. The first is the fear of death. Those with panic disorders or hypochondria often start catastrophizing when they feel their heart race or have shortness of breath. They might be stuck in traffic but fear that being alone in a tunnel or the mountains means the tunnel or cliff might suddenly collapse and they will die in the rubble.

The second fear is bankruptcy. Failing one promotion exam makes people think they will never pass the exam. A rebuke from a boss leads them to think they'll be passed over for promotions or get fired, eventually picturing themselves jobless and bankrupt.

The third fear is separation. After a breakup or an argument, they wonder if the conflict was caused by a flaw in their personality. They worry that they will never have a decent social life and will spend the rest of their lives without friends or love.

Lastly, there is the fear of losing attractiveness. A single gray hair, a pimple, or a wrinkle can trigger despair. They believe they've lost their youth or beauty and succumb to hopelessness.

If you're feeling discouraged right now, ask yourself what you're truly afraid of. If you're despondent after a breakup, ask yourself what you think will happen next. If illness has you worried, ponder what future events you fear.

Today's Exercise for Healthy
Self-Esteem: Name Your Fear

The first step to overcoming fear is acceptance. Acknowledge that you've suffered because of your habit of premature despair. Then accept what you truly fear.

Now consider what you're really afraid of. A student retaking exams might fear that they'll be stuck in this cycle forever. As mentioned before, ask yourself, *What do I think will happen next?* and repeat this question. Will you fail again next year? What if your parents are disappointed? What if your friends leave? Keep asking, *What will happen next?*

Eventually you'll identify your fundamental fear. Then, say it out loud: *I am afraid of dying alone/going broke/losing my looks/growing old.* By vocalizing your fear, you can then strategize how to address it. You might decide to work on maintaining your looks, earning more money, or taking care of your health. If there's no solution, at least you can accept it with *Well, there's nothing I can do about that.*

Incidentally, the friend who despaired during the football game feared being disappointed after expecting too much. He avoided hope to avoid disappointment. I, on the other hand, prefer to hold on to hope, even if it means facing disappointment later.

CHAPTER 24

The Habit of Lethargy

Lethargy goes by many names: laziness, lack of motivation, not wanting to do anything, weakness of will, and lack of perseverance. Lethargy is a major reason for self-criticism, perhaps due to the emphasis on diligence and hard work in agrarian cultures. Even in today's IT-driven society, many still view lethargy as a vice.

However, lethargy isn't a simple issue to tackle. There are numerous illnesses that can cause this symptom. It can arise from depression or withdrawal symptoms from addiction. Decreased hormone function can also result in a lack of motivation. Therefore, if lethargy persists for more than two weeks, it's essential to visit a doctor for a checkup. Lethargy shouldn't be merely endured or criticized; it could be a physical illness.

In this section, we'll focus on nonphysical causes of lethargy and explore how to handle it psychologically.

Motivation with Carrots,
Recovery Like a Rubber Band

Two forces drive humans: the carrot and the stick. Motivation primarily comes from the carrot. While one way to live is by avoiding the stick, that approach is too harsh. We endure the hardships of daily life thanks to the carrot, the positive reward that brings smiles and alleviates fatigue. For some parents, a handwritten card from their child reading "Mom and Dad, I love you" is the carrot. For some office workers, weekend getaways are their carrot. Positive rewards are like fuel. They give us new strength when we're tired and losing motivation. Studying hard and seeing your grades improve spark hope and energy to keep studying, especially if someone offers a word of praise.

But when the results aren't good, we feel disappointed and discouraged. Studying hard but not seeing your grades improve or receiving criticism instead of praise lowers your morale and makes you want to give up. If you stay up all night preparing a proposal and don't receive a word of appreciation from your boss, it's demoralizing. If you give a present to your mother-in-law and don't get the reaction you hoped for, it's disheartening, leading you to think, *Why do I even bother?* Couples who have been fighting for a long time often believe there is no hope of recovery. They lack the motivation to start marriage counseling, or if they do go, they often say, "What's the point? We've tried everything, and nothing will change."

There is always hope in the beginning. Everyone has a

certain degree of resilience, the ability to bounce back to their original state of motivation, like a rubber band. But when disappointments keep piling up, at some point, like an overstretched rubber band, that resilience snaps and the chance of recovery starts to look slim.

Learned Helplessness

Few people become lethargic after just one failure. We all have persistence and grit. But if we fail over and over or a significant failure leaves us deeply scarred, lethargy can set in.

This phenomenon of coming to expect failure as a result of repeated discouraging outcomes is called learned helplessness. Take a student who wants to achieve good grades. They study all night but fail the test, take online courses but still fail, and even with the help of a tutor, they fail again. This leads to the belief that *No matter how hard I try, I'll fail.* This mindset sets in before they even take the next test.

In sports, some teams seem to lose repeatedly despite having decent players. Coaches fear consecutive losses the most. When a team keeps losing, the entire team succumbs to learned helplessness. They begin to see themselves as a losing team full of losers. They don't feel motivated to perform their best because they believe they'll lose anyway, even slacking off during practice. They enter games already feeling defeated, unable to perform their best physically in their dejected mental state, leading to more losses. This cycle of defeat and learned helplessness is tough to break.

By understanding these dynamics, we can start addressing the root causes of lethargy, working toward breaking free from the cycle of learned helplessness and regaining motivation and resilience.

Three Situations That Cause Lethargy

Lethargy Factor 1: When Negative Rewards Overwhelm You

People who lose motivation and become lethargic haven't always experienced constant failure. Students who attend prestigious universities, young people who land jobs at top companies after fierce competition, and competent team leaders in companies can suddenly lose confidence. A workaholic can turn as lethargic as someone who has faced a lifetime of defeat.

The primary reason for falling into lethargy often stems from the issue of rewards. Rewards can be categorized into positive and negative. Positive rewards are the pleasant events that motivate us to act, such as promotions, salary increases, and praise or attention from others. On the other hand, negative rewards include failures, rejections, indifference, and discouraging reactions from those around us. No matter how many positive rewards one receives, if negative rewards have bigger emotional impact, one loses motivation. This often occurs in midlife, when people begin to feel that life is pointless and their achievements are meaningless.

If someone who was thriving suddenly loses motivation, they've likely encountered a significant negative reward. An example could be someone who had a stable job, supported their family, and thought they were living a happy life, only to find out they have a serious health issue or family problems. This leads to a complete loss of motivation and a sudden plunge into lethargy.

Lethargy Factor 2: Burnout Syndrome

Another common scenario involves people who become completely drained and lose motivation. This is known as burnout syndrome. In these cases, lethargy isn't necessarily related to rewards, positive or negative. To others, there may not seem to be any reason for their exhaustion.

This is primarily a physical issue. Regardless of how many positive rewards they receive mentally, relying on these rewards and overworking can deplete their physical energy within three to seven years. They become so absorbed in the "carrot" that they fail to realize they are running on empty.

In this case, taking a break usually resolves the issue. If possible, taking a sabbatical is ideal, but if that's not feasible, taking a vacation is advisable. If even that cannot be arranged, a restful weekend is crucial. Supplementing with vitamins, ensuring proper sleep, and maintaining a balanced diet are essential for recovery.

If burnouts recur or have a severe impact on your life, there are two things you ought to check. First, make sure you are in good physical health, especially looking for thyroid issues, which can cause extreme fluctuations in motivation. A simple blood test or ultrasound at the hospital can help identify this. Second, make sure you are getting enough sleep. Even the most motivated person can succumb to burnout after more than three days without adequate sleep.

Lethargy Factor 3: High Anxiety

Another contributing factor is mental health. People who are generally anxious expend their energy quickly. Constantly imagining worst-case scenarios and having numerous negative thoughts drain mental energy. Anxiety is easier to withstand when you are younger, but the body can no longer keep up with such prolonged exposure to stress as we approach middle age. Seek counseling or take medication to correct these anxious habits as soon as possible.

Misconceptions That Reinforce Lethargy

When people suddenly lose motivation, they try to find the reason behind their stagnation. They wonder, *Why am I like this? Is it an unresolved childhood trauma? Is it because I'm not pursuing my true desires? Is it a personality flaw? Do I lack role models?* Various thoughts come to mind.

The brain of someone with diminished motivation is busy, especially in the right hemisphere, which deals with profound and fundamental questions concerning cause and effect and what lies beneath the surface. Philosophers and astronomers probing the universe's origins often have a highly developed right brain.

However, these deep-thinking patterns can solidify into misconceptions that reinforce lethargy. While deep thinking is beneficial, it becomes problematic if it leads to increased lethargy. The misconceptions that exacerbate lethargy are as follows: First, believing that one must eliminate the cause of the lost motivation to move forward. Loss of motivation or lethargy can be compared to a football hitting a roadblock. While removing the roadblock is necessary, it doesn't guarantee the ball will start to roll again on its own. Second, thinking that one must feel excitement to regain motivation. Excitement typically comes from learning or doing something new, but repetitive tasks, even if not initially exciting, can become motivating through mastery and the comfort it brings. Third, assuming that one can only move when motivated. Whether motivated or not, one can take action and action can sometimes generate motivation. It's like pushing a car to start it; movement can lead to motivation.

Athletes, who are highly wary of lethargy, often see motivational slogans in gyms or sports equipment stores. I once saw the slogan "Don't cry. Don't complain. Just work" at a boxing gym. Nike's version, Just Do It, is another example. Motivation isn't a prerequisite for action.

Just Get Moving

French psychiatrist Christophe André once said, "Not taking action is typical of people with low self-esteem. They think, *If only this or that were different, I would act.* This entrenches a negative tendency and reinforces lethargy with the belief *It's a good thing I didn't act; it wouldn't have worked out anyway.*

Inaction, negative attitudes, and avoidance tendencies reinforce each other, creating a vicious cycle. The relationship between cause and effect is not linear but a destructive loop where one feeds the other. This argument holds considerable credibility. Many people believe they can start anew only after their negative attitudes and impulse to avoid disappear. They think they need to correct past experiences to change the present.

It's okay to do nothing. Not wanting to go to work right now isn't a problem. Lacking the desire to make money is fine. The issue is overthinking. This exhausts the brain, which then generates negative thoughts. To break free from lethargy, one must start moving. It doesn't matter if you don't want to or find it boring and pointless. Going outside for a short walk or even just light stretching is essential.

If you're unsure about getting married, start by dating. If dating seems daunting, go on a blind date. If that's too much, watch a movie with a friend. If you're hesitant about starting a marathon, take a lap around the neighborhood. Make small attempts toward your goal before deciding you will fail.

To regain motivation, stop thinking and start moving. It might not work initially, but move anyway. Turn your head from side to side, shake your arms. Don't wait for motivation to suddenly appear.

Today's Exercise for Healthy Self-Esteem: Stretching

Humans sleep daily, during which they might enter a state of wanting to stay still. While motivation disappears at night, it should reappear in the morning.

You don't need to start with strenuous physical activities. You're not aiming for something extraordinary right now. If you want to change lethargic habits, start by changing your posture. Rotate your neck and sit up straight. You'll feel better. Even if you don't immediately gain motivation, it's okay. Try light physical activities and do it often. Put down this book and take a short walk now.

CHAPTER 25

The Habit of the Inferiority Complex

The term *yeolpok*—Korean slang for "exploding sense of inferiority" or "explosion of fury"—comes up frequently online. It's often used derisively when someone gets emotional during a disagreement, like saying, *Look at you, having a yeolpok!*

Everyone Has an Inferiority Complex

Inferiority is an explosive emotion. If you want to provoke someone, just bring up something they lack. Perhaps each of us carries a bomb of inferiority within our hearts. A boss who gets upset over a subordinate's silly joke, a perfectly eligible person who is afraid to go on dates—many people harbor feelings of inferiority in ways we may not expect. Even those who are socially successful and envied by everyone can suffer from it.

An inferiority complex isn't inherently bad. It can drive us to acknowledge our shortcomings and motivate us to improve. However, when we believe that we are essentially inferior, it takes a toll on our self-esteem and happiness.

Problems also arise when we see ourselves as inferior for no good reason. For example, I once knew a student who worried that people might make fun of her for being short. On the contrary, her cohorts found her adorable and charming. It is indeed unfortunate when we are ashamed of our strengths and try to hide them, mistaking them for shortcomings.

The Three Thoughts That Make Up an Inferiority Complex

Usually, one emotion is linked to one thought. When we think we are exploited, we feel a sense of injustice. When we think we are deceived, we feel betrayed. In contrast, the emotion of inferiority is linked to a combination of three thoughts.

The first thought is the belief that you have short-comings. Everyone has shortcomings. Acknowledging your weaknesses can lead to humility and peace of mind. However, when two misconceptions also enter the mix, a feeling of inferiority sets in.

The first misconception is that everyone else has what you lack. This is often called a sense of inadequacy. There's a difference between not having something and being the only one without it. When gripped by this thought, you can't view others objectively and feel unjustly disadvantaged from the start.

The second misconception is that you suffer significant harm because of your shortcomings. This feeling is similar to having a complex. For instance, someone might attribute their unemployment solely to personal shortcomings or to the challenges they have faced in life, whether that be a difficult childhood, the divorce of their parents, or discrimination based on their appearance. This thought includes a component of aggression toward others.

Inferiority is a complex emotion—a mix of feelings of inadequacy, a sense of injustice, and victimhood. This mix is like an overinflated balloon, ready to burst at any moment.

Once on Top, Now Struggling

The "terrible sixes" refers to the time when children start to defy their parents more frequently. They become determined to do everything adults do, often with a strong-willed attitude. During this period, children are armed with a sense of omnipotence, the complete opposite of inferiority. This phase is characterized by an overinflated sense of competence. While it can be a challenging time for parents, it is a completely normal stage in a child's development.

During the omnipotent period, children often see themselves as equal to or even superior to adults, sometimes viewing themselves as supernatural beings. They might wear capes and pretend to be Superman, boast about being the best singer in the world, or insist on being the princess in a game and demand that others follow their rules. It is common for children in this age group to argue frequently because everyone wants to be the leader.

Parents often become anxious during this period that their child's boasting might become a problem and that the child might face significant disappointment when confronted with reality. Parents may feel the need to prepare their child for the harshness of the world, to immunize them against future frustrations.

However, it is important to be cautious about crushing this sense of omnipotence too harshly, as it can leave a lasting scar. When a child experiences an event that reveals their limitations, the resulting disappointment can become deeply ingrained. If this feeling becomes fixed, the child may have intense emotional reactions every time they encounter their limits later in life.

The omnipotent period is typically when one's earliest memories are from. The tastes of the foods they ate and the joyful moments they experienced can remain as cherished memories. Conversely, if their sense of omnipotence is crushed, it can leave a lasting wound. Resentment toward parents may linger, with thoughts like *Even a hedgehog loves its offspring. Did my parents really have to be so brutally honest with me?* This can lead to enduring feelings of inadequacy, where the child grows up thinking, *I'm really no good. If I show any confidence, I'll end up being an outcast forever,* thus, discouraging themselves and assuming the role of second fiddle for the rest of their lives.

Can an Inferiority Complex Fuel Success?

As mentioned earlier, an inferiority complex is a powerful, explosive emotion that can sometimes be harnessed as a resource for success. For example, in weight loss challenge programs, coaches might motivate participants by highlighting their weaknesses, pushing them to change their appearance and personality. This approach might work on some participants, but it can also lead to frustration and result in their quitting.

This method brings to mind the harsh pedagogical style of old-school teachers or personal trainers, who would provoke their students into learning. The teacher would motivate students by berating them: "Your parents aren't rich and you're not good-looking. If you don't study hard and get into a good school, you'll have nothing!" Martial arts films often feature sensei who accuse their apprentices of having no talent, starve them, exploit their labor, and make them want it bad enough to throw themselves into the training. In the days when patriarchal and tyrannical pedagogical styles were considered legitimate, the teachers who took on the role of abuser were respected. Students feared and disliked the teacher while they were at school but looked back on their school days later after they'd achieved success and were grateful to the teacher.

While such techniques were once celebrated, they're seen as risky today. Encouragement and support are now deemed more important. Triggering a student's inferiority complex can lead to internal explosions rather than fuel success. No matter how intimidating the teacher, a student might simply say, "So what if I'm a loser? Leave me alone!"

People with low self-esteem sometimes seek out people who can give them tough love, believing they are weak and in need of strong guidance. In therapy, they might say, "Just tell me what to do. Don't ask questions, just give instructions for me to follow." This approach might help them achieve their short-term goals but damages their self-esteem, causing an inferiority complex to resurface when they feel disrespected. Happiness and self-esteem can't flourish under constant feelings of inadequacy.

The Inferiority Complex of Successful People

Even among those who are deemed successful, there are individuals who struggle to shed their inferiority complex. Despite receiving praise and admiration, they often dismiss it as mere politeness or flattery.

These individuals typically do not feel the need to get past their sense of inferiority because they equate it with humility. They believe that shedding their sense of inferiority would be arrogant and make them unlikable. Although they recognize the issues caused by their acute sensitivity to inferiority triggers, they fear that they will be disliked and ostracized if they shed their sense of inferiority and become confident.

When a person's inferiority complex motivates them to achieve their goals, they find it hard to let go of the sense of inferiority. They cling to seemingly insignificant aspects of their past—such as their less-than-ideal family background, their impoverished childhood, or lack of affection—as if these experiences still define them. Their inferiority complex has been both a driving force and a whip, pushing them to study hard or work tirelessly to escape hardship. Despite having a comfortable and satisfying life, they struggle to let go of the habit of belittling themselves.

People with ambiguous types of inferiority complexes also find it difficult to let go. They pressure themselves with thoughts like *I've never felt true love, I'm not particularly good at anything, I don't have the stability that others do,* or *I have low self-esteem.* The things they believe they lack are often things most people don't possess, either. Concepts like finding true love, being exceptionally good at something, having the stability that others have, or self-esteem others lack are often vague and subjective. They lack a clear definition, making it difficult to tell if or when you've obtained it.

Thus, if you believe you have a problem, you need to examine its meaning carefully. Reflect on what exactly you think you lack and whether it's a genuine shortcoming. Consider what you gain from holding on to your inferiority complex. There is a reason for every habit you've developed, and if you haven't been able to let go of your inferiority complex, you need to understand what it means to you.

Letting Go of Your Sense of Inferiority

Inferiority is a "hot" emotion, a mixture of inadequacy, self-reproach, shame, and victimhood that torments us. It makes one's heart race and one's face flush, agitating both mind and body.

In your twenties and early thirties, we find it hard to distinguish feelings of inferiority from passion, as it can also be a source of energy. Many people work hard to overcome their feelings of inadequacy and achieve success, be it professional or personal. Some study hard to overcome a major flaw, while others strive to develop enough charm to compensate for their weaknesses.

However, as you reach middle age, it's time to let go of your inferiority complex. Carrying feelings of self-reproach and victimhood will eventually take a toll, especially on your health. As we grow older, our hearts and lungs can no longer handle such intense emotions. It is physically taxing to always be conscious of other people's opinions and worrying that one does not measure up. Those who suffer from an inferiority complex begin to seek medical help past their thirties when their bodies are no longer able to handle the hot emotion, causing symptoms of heart palpitations and insomnia.

Some people turn to alcohol to soothe the pain caused by their inferiority complex. This attempt to take the edge off turns into alcohol dependency, which damages the heart and liver. Those who attend rehabilitation centers often struggle to concentrate during therapy sessions and reveal an added inferiority complex about their inability to control their drinking.

Ancient Thought Can Offer a Modern Remedy

The belief that you are inferior stems from a world view that divides things into superior and inferior. People who feel insecure about their educational background often judge others based on their educational backgrounds. For those who feel inferior about being poor, the world is divided into the haves and the have-nots. This mindset is largely the result of social and environmental factors rather than the individual's fault.

To fundamentally root out your inferiority complex, you must break the habit of categorizing people and things into superior or inferior, good or bad. The philosophies of Laozi and Zhuangzi emphasize this.* They highlight the futility of evaluating the world based on usefulness or value. In one of Zhuangzi's stories, a useless tree grows undisturbed because no one cuts it down, while useful trees are quickly felled. The useless tree, which does not boast, survives and

---

* Laozi (born sixth century BC) and Zhuangzi (born fourth century BC) were notable Chinese philosophers central in the development of Daoism, or Taoism, which emphasizes union with nature and the pursuit of simplicity. Both explored their ideas through the rejection of dichotomies, embracing intentional contradictions and exploring the falsities of binaries.

becomes a community's guardian and offers shade for villagers to rest under.

I admire Laozi's and Zhuangzi's world view. As public sentiment grows more turbulent and polarization deepens, many find solace in their teachings, thinking, *What good is wealth and success?* Keeping an open mind and questioning the value systems that surround us can be a good way to calm an inferiority complex. If you have trouble controlling your temper due to your sense of inferiority or have a complex you wish to overcome, try reading Zhuangzi. This way of thinking can be a clean and simple defense mechanism.

Today's Exercise for Healthy Self-Esteem: Adopting the "Such Is Life" Attitude

A severe inferiority complex can raise your heart rate and cause shortness of breath, leading to an excess of oxygen in the blood. Contrary to popular belief, this is not beneficial and can cause numbness and stiffness in your limbs, potentially progressing to hyperventilation syndrome and fainting.

Letting go of your inferiority complex and regaining composure result in the opposite physical state: reduced heart rate and breathing rate, increased carbon dioxide pressure in the blood, and a relaxed state. While we cannot control our heart rate, we can regulate our breathing to some extent. Slow, deep breaths, particularly long exhales, help one to reach a calm state. This mimics the physiological state of those who have let go of their inferiority complex.

The breathing technique is simple. Count to three on the inhale and to seven on the exhale. Repeat this cycle. While exhaling, mentally say, "Such is life." Taking the world less seriously can help cool your inferiority complex. Over time, you'll realize there's nothing exceptionally good or bad in the world—just the pleasure of taking calming breaths. Such is life. Let's take life less seriously.

CHAPTER 26

The Habit of Procrastination and Avoidance

Many people have preconceived notions about emotional pain. They respond to it differently than they do to physical pain. In the past, even physical illnesses were often blamed on a lack of mental strength, but this attitude has largely disappeared. However, when it comes to emotional pain, many still think it results from a lack of willpower or a personality flaw. Adults often criticize or blame young people who are emotionally hurting, saying things like "You were spoiled by your parents" or "Why are you struggling with something so trivial?"

As a result, even when people seek treatment, they hesitate to share how much they are suffering, what is causing their pain, and how distressed they are. For example, a wife whose husband has cheated may feel unable to express her emotional turmoil even though she has done nothing wrong.

Young People Who Can't
Say They're Hurting

Young adults are no different. They avoid talking about how lonely and exhausted they feel and instead make excuses. As a doctor, I am not here to judge or criticize, but they still feel the need to justify themselves. They say things like "I'm usually very strong-willed and positive," or "I've tried so hard to stay positive. I have even embraced faith and I'm reading a lot of books." Then they ask, "Why do I still have low self-esteem? Is it because of how my parents raised me? But that can't be fixed here, can it?"

The sad part is that their excessive focus on the cause drains the energy they need to solve the problem. They don't pay attention to what emotions they are experiencing or how long they've been struggling with insomnia, for example. They fail to identify and address what's making them suffer and instead get mired in finding the cause.

Many people fear entering the stage of change because they don't want to admit they are emotionally wounded. They feel that admitting this means admitting defeat and opening themselves up to criticism, so they deflect the main issue by bringing up irrelevant questions and concerns in therapy sessions. This resistance to change leads them to delay solutions, skirting around the real issues and failing to embark on the path to recovery and transformation.

Three Patterns of Avoidance

People don't consciously think, *I'll avoid solving my problem because I'm afraid of criticism.* Before such worries can even arise, they preemptively focus on other tasks. Those who avoid confronting their emotional pain often exhibit three common themes:

Observing Others

During counseling, just hearing "You're not the only one. Others feel this way, too" can ease the client's mind. People experiencing emotional crises hope that they are not the only ones experiencing the problem. They seek confirmation that others also face such issues and that it isn't due to a lack of willpower or personality flaws. However, this habit can solidify, leading them to constantly observe others. They examine how others are doing at work, spend time at home checking social media to see how others live, and even when seeking help, they prioritize asking, "Are there others struggling like me?" over expressing their own feelings and desires for treatment.

Investigating the Cause

Accepting one's emotional pain does not always lead to relieving it because one can become obsessed with identifying the cause of the pain. People scrutinize whether it was a poor choice they made, childhood trauma, or a dysfunctional relationship with their parents. Typically, these individuals have read several psychology books before seeking help. The problem is that the common answer to such pain is "the past," which cannot be changed. Relationships with parents, childhood wounds, past actions, and inherited traits may be identified, but they remain unalterable.

Identifying the cause is the start of solving psychological problems, not the end goal. Striving for perfect understanding is futile; instead, energy should be reserved for addressing your current situation and planning future actions. Ultimately, there are no definitive and fundamental causes. Understanding the real cause can sometimes help heal the pain and prevent future issues, but remaining fixated on the cause hinders progress toward resolution.

Complaining and Assigning Blame

Complaining and assigning blame yields nothing. Venting to friends might provide temporary emotional relief, but it doesn't change anything. It is especially damaging when directed at family, as it places stress on relationships and exacerbates emotional distress.

When we manage to stop blaming and denouncing others, the blame often turns inward. Whether obsessively blaming ourselves or others, the time spent on this detracts from finding solutions.

Four Prerequisites for Problem-Solving

To heal a wounded heart and break bad habits, you must embrace change. If you want to reclaim your self-esteem, focus your energy on transforming your future rather than on analyzing your past. Shed the habit of avoiding and delaying change, and set new goals. Here are four prerequisites for this process.

Prioritize Your Heart

The agent of change is you, and the target of change is also you. We spend too much time in misery comparing ourselves to others, arguing, or self-blaming. Start by caring for your own heart. Identify what hurts you the most and think about how to heal it. Painful experiences like school bullying, criticism and violence at home, or workplace harassment are all deeply distressing. Dedicate yourself to transforming and healing your heart. Reflect on your current emotional state and how you want it to change.

Take Action

We are on a path to building healthy self-esteem. The fundamental goal of this book is to heal and restore self-esteem. This process doesn't always happen in the mind alone. Merely thinking about it won't change anything. You need to read books, write, speak, draw, or exercise if necessary. Change begins with action.

Persevere

The next chapter will suggest actions to restore self-esteem. As you follow them, you might find them uninteresting or feel negative emotions creeping in. Thoughts like *What's the point?* or *Will this really help my self-esteem?* or *I've tried this before* might occur. Still, persevere. The journey to revitalizing self-esteem is like going on a diet. Initially, you lose weight quickly, but then the weight loss slows down. People often become discouraged and lose motivation at this point, doubting if they will continue to progress. This is entirely natural. Everything is exciting and enjoyable at first, but becomes less interesting over time, whether it's learning to cook or paint. One must cross this threshold to progress from novice to veteran.

You will encounter this plateau in your journey to regain self-esteem. And when you do, don't stop or take a break from the effort; stick with the exercises. This is the stage where you become accustomed to your stronger self-esteem, and with continued practice, you'll manage your emotions better.

Work Together, Not Alone

Rebuilding your self-esteem doesn't have to be boring and tedious. Do not make yourself miserable. To overcome and persist, it's better to do it together rather than alone.

Rebuilding self-esteem is similar to physical training. One of the hardest things in the world, I believe, is finding the motivation to work out at the gym regularly. In the past, people went to the gym and worked out alone. Nowadays, many people train with personal trainers or participate in group classes. Working out in groups provides more fun and motivation than doing it alone.

The same goes for mental health training. It's more efficient to do it together, preferably with professional help rather than just with other individuals. If it's difficult to work with others, use tools like a journal, blog, or notebook. Instead of letting your daily efforts pass by unnoticed, record what you did and how you did it.

Today's Exercise for Healthy Self-Esteem: Set a Specific Role Model

Decide what kind of person you want to become by solving your current problems. Setting goals is different from complaining or self-criticism. Think of it as drawing a blueprint for a house. Designing the house isn't about recognizing how cramped and uncomfortable your current home is. It's about planning the details of the house you want to live in, considering space and flow. Similarly, when setting goals, clearly define the person you want to be, the main emotions you are feeling, and what actions to take.

To clearly set your goals, follow these three steps:

Step 1. List your dissatisfactions with yourself.

For example:

I hate my boss's criticism. This is dissatisfaction with someone else, not yourself.

I hate that I lose sleep over how much I despise my boss.

Step 2. Write down who you want to be instead.

For example:

I want to erase memories of my childhood. The past cannot be changed, nor can memories be forcibly erased.

I resent myself for choosing this job. This is about the past and self-criticism. It's better suited for Step 1.

I want to focus on myself after work and stop being preoccupied with how much I hate my boss. This reflects current dissatisfaction but sets a specific goal for the future.

Step 3. Describe how the person from Step 2 would handle situations from Step 1.

For example:

I want to be like my colleague who remains unfazed by the boss's criticism. He immerses himself in hobbies and does not think about work when he's out of the office.

Once you've set a concrete goal, move on to the next step, which is to take action. If you want to be like your coworker who shakes off criticisms right away, take action and do as he does.

CHAPTER 27

The Habit of Sensitivity

Our minds are like our skin. Biologically, brain tissue and skin originate from the same ectoderm layer. The healing process for both is remarkably similar. Imagine continuously pricking one spot on your skin with a sharp object. It will become inflamed and swollen, and even the slightest touch will cause pain and discomfort.

The mind reacts similarly. When we experience stress, that part of our minds becomes sensitive. For example, children who grow up with a drunk and violent father may develop an intense aversion to middle-aged men drinking. Sensitivity is the first noticeable reaction caused by emotional wounds or anxiety. Regardless of the cause, prolonged sensitivity can have a negative impact on how we relate to others.

Faulty Connections

Everyone faces unfortunate events in life—getting hurt, being betrayed, losing something valuable, or simply being disappointed. Strong self-esteem helps individuals remain resilient. They don't let adverse events weaken their self-esteem. While difficult experiences inevitably impact them, they don't let those experiences reshape their lives. It's like having a solid defense between oneself and bad events, similar to how antibodies fight viruses.

However, those with low self-esteem often link many things to themselves. They have a cognitive pattern that connects life's bad events to themselves, which generates feelings of guilt. They blame themselves for the misfortunes of those around them. Parents of sick children often suffer from depression due to overwhelming self-blame. Children from troubled marriages experience various psychological issues stemming from unfounded guilt that they are to blame for their parents' fights.

The problem starts with these connections. Self-blame happens when you find the cause of others' issues within yourself. Anger erupts when you blame your problems on others. When we take everything so personally, it sows the seeds of sensitivity and hurts our self-esteem.

Are They Talking About Me?

The belief that irrelevant occurrences are related to you is referred to as an idea of reference. This pattern triggers various emotions that intertwine with thoughts and further complicate emotions. As thoughts increase, so do emotions, leading to heightened sensitivity.

As mentioned, the sensitivity of the mind mirrors the sensitivity of skin. Injured skin becomes sensitive, feeling pain from stimuli that previously went unnoticed. Similarly, when we are emotionally sensitive, we react strongly to minor stimuli. Thus comments or specific expressions from others stay with us for longer and can bother us.

People with healthy self-esteem do not concern themselves with matters that are irrelevant to them. Those with low self-esteem and high sensitivity, however, cling to and ruminate on unnecessary information. They delve into its meaning and underlying motives, pondering how it relates to them.

For instance, in a social gathering, someone might brag about buying land in the countryside and making a fortune from its redevelopment. A person with healthy self-esteem might outwardly express mild envy but won't dwell on it. However, someone with low self-esteem might think, *Did they say that to spite me, knowing I'm having financial problems?* They'll ruminate on this incident for days.

When we are struggling emotionally, we tend to overthink the small things and make great personal mountains out of others' tiny molehills.

An Idea of Reference Becomes a Persecutory Idea

While not as severe as a delusion, an idea of reference can torment those with fragile minds due to its persistent nature. It stems from a lack of self-trust, leading to doubts about one's defensive capabilities. This fear of not recovering from emotional setbacks causes constant worry.

Those caught in an idea of reference often ponder how

to appear more confident, indicating their lack of self-assurance. They become hyperaware of subtle comments and observations in social interactions. This focus on the remarks of others might make it seem like they have good memories, as they dwell on minor issues long after others have moved on. Months later, they might call someone to confront them about a comment made in passing: *Why did you say that about me in front of everyone?*

When an idea of reference intensifies in one's mind, it evolves into a persecutory idea, commonly known as paranoia. This condition exhausts everyone involved, with the individual constantly worrying about being wronged or excluded.

Leave Others' Emotions to Them

To get past oversensitivity, start by distinguishing between yourself and others. The scope of others is vast. Everyone besides you yourself falls in the category of others—your family, friends, and coworkers.

Frequent conflicts between parents and children arise when they forget this distinction. Because parents give life to their children and raise them, they often mistake the children as extensions of themselves, leading to meddling and nagging. Similarly, children take it for granted that their parents will always support them and make sacrifices for them. Their parents ought to trust them and be devoted to them. However, parents are humans, too. They are individuals who have struggled through life and are now becoming more vulnerable as they grow older.

When children mature, they no longer see their parents solely as "my mom and dad." A mature child recognizes that their parents are aging. They acknowledge that their parents are turning into elderly folk with declining health and worsening memory who are becoming sadder and more suspicious. They see their parents as individuals with emotions and needs, just like everyone else.

For the sake of our own happiness, we must cultivate the habit of leaving others' concerns to them. It's impossible to be happy while ruminating on what others have said or done, feeling victimized by their actions.

Of course, this doesn't mean we should be indifferent to everything. Cooperation is necessary in the world, and it is essential to offer interest and affection to the people we love. However, it is key to let others deal with their own emotions. Each person has their unique triggers and emotional responses, which is why people may laugh or cry at different parts of the same film. It is therefore unproductive to ask someone, "Why are you upset over something like that?" Their emotions are theirs alone, and we cannot and should not try to change them. Their emotions are not caused by us and are not our responsibility.

If you want to help someone, go ahead. But don't try to change their emotions or take their feelings on as your own. If someone is angry or suspicious, that's their business. You don't need to become angry with them, nor should you let their emotional response influence yours. Their emotions are theirs.

Today's Exercise for Healthy Self-Esteem:
Mantras to Reduce Oversensitivity

When you look closely, there aren't many things in the world worth fighting for with all your might. Most disputes start over trivial matters, like bumping into someone or not being addressed respectfully.

Does it truly matter who said or did what? Is it necessary to lose your mind over people you dislike or are of little consequence to you? When you find yourself becoming easily irritated in relationships, say aloud, "So what if things turn a bit sour with them?" If you're overly worried about your health, try saying, "So what if I feel a bit ill? Everyone experiences pain and ill health from time to time." All it takes is these simple words to help reduce sensitivity.

When we repeatedly obsess over something, it's called a fixation. To break free from it, tell yourself, *What's the big deal?* If you've made a poor financial decision and lost money, remember that fixating on the loss is more harmful than the lost amount itself. Obsessing over the loss wastes time and damages relationships. Tell yourself, *What's a few bucks lost?* When going through a breakup, try saying to yourself, *What's the big deal? It's just a breakup.* You'll find that the thoughts weighing heavy on your heart start to lighten.

Mantras:
What's the big deal?
So what?
These things happen!

Accept, Want, Pretend, Sustain

To break a bad habit, you need to go through the following four steps.

Accept

The first step is to accept two things. One, that you have a bad habit, and two, that this habit is causing you distress. To facilitate this acceptance, it is helpful to write it down and read it out loud. For example, write the first line as "I have a habit of trying to change and control others' emotions." The next line could be: "This habit is exhausting." Keep these written lines and read them aloud frequently. If you want to quit smoking, write: "I have a habit of smoking. This habit is harmful to my body." Read it aloud many times. The reason people often resume smoking after deciding to quit is that they forget these two facts. Forgetting that smoking is an addiction leads to thoughts like *I can smoke just once and then quit again.* Forgetting that the habit is harmful makes you think, *It's better to smoke than to be stressed.* Thus you must continuously remind your brain, for at least a week, that you have a habit and that it is harmful to you.

Want

Every habit has its dual nature. The same goes for bad habits. While you want to break the habit, there is also a fear that your life will unravel without it. To completely break a bad habit, you must want it badly enough. Everyone has habits that lower their self-esteem, and you must truly want to escape from them.

Pretend

It would be ideal if the desire for change began deep within your heart, allowing you to quit easily. However, such cases are rare. Until the new habit is formed, you need to pretend you've already broken the old one. Pretending until it becomes real takes at least two months.

Sustain

This is the most challenging part for those with low self-esteem. Habits have a tendency to recur. Thus complete change does not happen after one attempt. The problem arises when you relapse and think, *I knew I couldn't do it. Look, I've failed again,* leading to despair. Keep at it.

Change is not achieved through a single decision or attempt. It involves many attempts and failures. Falling back into feelings of inferiority or reverting to bad habits is a natural part of the process. The important thing is not to conclude that you have failed. You must continually rebuild and reinforce, as only then can your mind reach completion.

Self-Esteem Class Summary

- The more developed a civilization, the greater the number of stress factors.
- Asking "What do you think will happen next?" is a good means of exposing core fears. Once you identify what you're worried about, you often find that the problem is manageable.
- Rest is mandatory for physical and emotional recovery.
- Don't let lethargy stop you from taking action. Make small attempts toward your goal before deciding you will fail. Overthinking merely exhausts the brain, which generates negative thoughts.
- Happiness and self-esteem can't flourish under constant feelings of inadequacy.
- Inferiority is a hot emotion comprised of inadequacy, self-reproach, shame, and victimhood that torment us. However, it can also be a source of energy.
- If you believe you have a problem, you need to examine its meaning carefully. There is a reason for every habit you've developed, and if you haven't been able to let go of your inferiority complex, you need to understand what it means to you.

- To fundamentally root out your inferiority complex, you must break the habit of categorizing people and things into superior or inferior.
- Taking the world less seriously can help cool your inferiority complex.
- People who avoid confronting their emotional pain often exhibit three common themes: observing others, investigating the cause, and complaining and assigning blame.
- Four prerequisites for problem-solving are: prioritize your heart, take action, persevere, and work together, not alone.
- The sensitivity of the mind mirrors the sensitivity of the skin. When we are emotionally sensitive, we react strongly to minor stimuli.
- Three mantras to repeat when certain situations cause sensitivity are: *What's the big deal? So what?* and *These things happen!*

PART 6

Things to Overcome for Self-Esteem Recovery

CHAPTER 28

Overcoming Wounds

Farmers sow seeds in the spring. In the summer, they pull out weeds and spray pesticides to control pests. The process of recovering self-esteem is similar.

We are reading this book to harvest the fruit of self-esteem. The earlier chapters correspond to the spring and summer phases. Understanding what self-esteem is and recognizing what it means to respect and love oneself is the work of spring. In the summer, we remove obstacles.

In nature, simply removing harmful things yields results. Crops grow if we remove the pests, and chicks hatch on their own when protected from predators. Self-esteem also follows this principle to some extent. If you remove the bad things that harm your mind, recovery becomes easier.

Knowing what is bad and harmful and accepting that you have such traits is the preliminary step for recovering self-esteem. The next step is knowing specific ways to overcome them and to practice these methods.

All Wounds Are in the Past

The first thing to examine is wounds. When we say, "I was wounded," what do we mean exactly? What can become a wound, and how does it come to be there? Many people wonder about this during counseling. I'll answer this in three ways.

Anything

Anything can become a wound. Any words, events, or actions can leave a wound. Therefore, asking, "Am I foolish for suffering for years over something like that?" is meaningless.

Any Way

Wounds are expressed in all sorts of ways. Some people cry, some get angry, some express it with laughter, and some clench their teeth. Some people live as if nothing happened, and some deny it ever happened.

Any Time

Some people show their wounds immediately after they occur, while for others, it may take years to surface. Some people are overwhelmed by the pain of their wounds decades later, while others start and finish the healing process quickly.

*

People often ask if their past wounds or traumas are affecting their current lives. My answer is always similar: "It might be, and it might not be." The way wounds occur and appear is so varied that there are no set rules. But there is an important commonality. All traumas are events that happened in the past. Think of it as a large picture of a frog. If you show a large picture of a frog to young children, they might be scared and step back or burst into tears. But the picture itself can never harm them. It's just that, in the moment when they fear the frog picture, the reassurance doesn't resonate with them.

Consequences of Trauma

There is a character named Jenny in the American TV show *The L Word*. Initially she appears as an ordinary character about to marry her boyfriend. Then she impulsively falls in love with a coffee shop owner, and after that, she shows extreme and self-destructive behavior. She alienates her friends, hurts them, and engages in self-harm.

Jenny, it turns out, has a wound from childhood sexual abuse. Her parents didn't protect young Jenny and covered up the incident. Moreover, they blamed everything on her. In this process, Jenny received additional wounds and had to live with the pain.

Jenny constantly writes and dreams of becoming a writer and falling in love with a decent man, but she cannot escape her dark memories. She even indulges in promiscuous sexual activities to forget the past, but it does not dull the pain. Eventually she goes on to become a dancer at a strip club. She performs shows in front of drunk and unruly men. When a friend eventually asks her, "Why are you doing this when you went through the things you did as a child?" Jenny replies, "Here I can stop when I want to. I can show as much as I want and stop where I want. I like that feeling."

What Is the Weak Spot in My Heart?

Wounds in the heart often leave traces. Time heals, but half-healed spots suddenly cause pain. Just when you think you've forgotten, the memory resurfaces and torments you. On the surface it seems healed, but inside it festers and becomes increasingly painful. Jenny's wound is the incident of sexual abuse. It's a past event, but the pain is ongoing. The unhealed wound continues to worsen and cause pain.

The sensitive part of the heart that smarts when irritated is called the "weak spot" in the heart. For Jenny, the weak spot is not feeling in control of herself. The inability to fight off or escape from the abuser left a devastating impact on her. And in the process of dealing with the incident, she couldn't oppose her parents' decision or defy their orders.

Everyone has a weak spot in their heart, and it is related to wounds experienced in the past. For someone wounded by sibling rivalry, competition becomes their weak spot. For someone with trauma from being falsely accused, the smallest accusation can trigger their weak spot. Each person's weak spot varies.

Defense Mechanisms to Protect the Weak Spot

People who are wounded are eager to protect their weak spots. They develop defense mechanisms more often than not unconsciously. One person may use multiple defense mechanisms, and various methods may be used for one event. Defense mechanisms are quite important in a person's life. Some argue that the type of defense mechanisms we use determines our personality or character.

Immature Defense vs. Mature Defense

Sometimes defense mechanisms that protect the weak spot harm the individual or other people. These are called immature defense mechanisms. In the aforementioned drama, Jenny wants to free herself from feeling out of control and activates a defense mechanism. However, her methods include self-harm, alcohol dependence, and promiscuity. These actions may seem comforting in the moment, but eventually lead to regret and negative consequences.

Other examples of immature defense mechanisms include criticism and self-blame. When negative feelings arise, some people may attack others, blame themselves, or gossip as a defense mechanism. For instance, if your mother-in-law says something hurtful to you, but you cannot acknowledge the fact that she hurt you, much less confront her about it, you might vent to your children or other members of your family. Although this doesn't harm the mother-in-law or you directly, it's not an effective defense. It also causes new conflicts between your children and their grandmother or between the family and the in-laws, creating tension.

Some people suppress their feelings, which often leads to misplacement of frustration. If they're angry at their husband, they might scold their child, saying, "You're just like your father!" The defense mechanism of suppression eventually erupts as anger and aggression, causing trouble for a lot of people.

In contrast, people with mature defense mechanisms protect their hearts without harming anyone. The representative of mature defense mechanisms is sublimation. This involves developing a negative event or related emotions into productive activities. For example, a teenager who experienced bullying and depression may grow up to become a psychological expert helping bullied students. Remembering their own frustrations and sadness makes them a compassionate therapist. Other examples include musicians who turn the pain of a breakup into songs or writers who express their wounds through literature. Rather than cause harm, these defense mechanisms help others.

The process of healing wounds and recovering self-esteem also includes developing mature defense mechanisms. With the warm empathy and advice of experts, one learns how to respond to pain and naturally finds ways to heal wounds. Even mature people have wounds and weak spots, but they find peaceful ways to protect themselves.

The Unchangeable Past, Now Safe

Two things in the world cannot be changed: others and the past. The wounds received in the past that remain until the present are painful for everyone. They are hard to forget. Unfortunately, the past cannot be changed or erased.

The reason why past wounds torment our present selves is that they distort our perception of time. They make something that ended long ago feel like it's happening now. I once counseled someone who had been robbed ten years earlier, and throughout the session, they kept looking at the door. When I asked why, they said, "It feels like the robber might come right through that door."

Wounds from parents in childhood, wounds from teachers, and bullying from friends are all in the past. The "me" who was neglected and belittled is "the me of long ago." But it feels as if the experience is ongoing in the present. The wounds are painful, but it's essential to remember that they are all in the past.

When the knots in the mind are sublimated, one can escape this confusion. It's confusing while it's in the mind, but once it's brought out, it becomes clear that it's all in the past. We've moved past it, and now we are safe. The adults who tormented us have grown old and we have become stronger. We need to realize that.

Telling the Brain: "It's All in the Past"

Our brain doesn't know that the pain is in the past. The brain is still confused. Even if it understands that the pain is in the past, it can lose its good judgment when we are drunk or unwell. It confuses the past with the present.

Wounds are like watching a horror movie. During the movie, ghosts and zombies scare us, making us cower and scream. But once the film is over and we leave the cinema, the fear we felt in the cinema has nothing to do with reality. We need to constantly inform the brain of this fact. We need to make sure the brain fully understands that the wound is in the past. For this, it's more effective to provide external information rather than just internal persuasion. The deep part of the brain, the center of emotion and memory, needs to hear it. We need to tell the brain out loud: "It's all in the past. I'm okay now. I'm safe now."

The brain will keep getting confused. Having thought wrongly for so long, the brain is reluctant to accept that it's all in the past. Thoughts like *What's the use of this method? It's pointless to mumble to myself that I'm okay. I'll do it later* will arise. The brain prefers familiarity, so it tries to maintain the distressing situation caused by the wound. What should we do? We must keep telling it, a hundred times a day, out loud, so the ears hear it continuously. That's how the ear cells, heart cells, and facial muscles come to receive and take in the message.

CHAPTER 29

Overcoming Resistance

Most romantic comedies start out with two people who seem mismatched who meet and keep becoming entwined. They gradually become closer, and it looks like they are falling for each other. But then, just as they are about to fall in love, an obstacle appears. One of them, typically the one with low self-esteem, will literally or figuratively communicate, "I don't know if I deserve this happiness" or "You're a wonderful person, but I'm not ready for love right now. I'll come back when I'm a better person." Then they disappear. Even though they dream of happiness, they doubt whether they truly deserve it and retreat.

The protagonist is charming and longs for love but has wounds and low self-esteem. So even when they find love, they can't cope with it. They want it, yet they also want to let it go. This ambivalence exists within us all.

Wanting but Not Wanting

When asked if we want our self-esteem to recover, most people would answer yes. But we need to think about whether, deep down, we truly want our lives to change. Surprisingly, the answer is not always straightforward. In reality, when asked this question, people sometimes say quite unexpected things:

> Yes, because I want my children to live in a happy world.
>
> Of course, because I need to get a job and get married.
>
> Obviously. Nobody wants to be unhappy. Why do you keep repeating the same question?

People read books and seek counseling to recover their self-esteem but often find themselves focusing on other goals. They focus on their children's issues rather than their own self-esteem. Or they worry about immediate tasks, which hinders their focus on recovery.

Our minds react ambivalently to the prospect of significant life changes like self-esteem recovery. We want it desperately, yet we don't want it, moving toward recovery while simultaneously engaging in opposing actions. We want change but resist it. To truly recover, we need to recognize and get past our resistance. Some might say, "There's no resistance in me, so just help me recover my self-esteem quickly." But understanding and addressing resistance is crucial in the recovery process.

Resistance is a natural phenomenon, much like the friction that occurs when moving an object. We all wish to move from an unhappy self to a happy self. But to move from here to there, we must overcome friction and inertia. There's always a force keeping us in place. It's more realistic to recognize what causes increased friction and learn how we can overcome resistance rather than denying its existence.

For example, if an interviewer asks a job applicant, "Do you want to work for this company?" all applicants would answer, "Yes, I want to." However, deep down, they might worry about not being able to sleep in or whether they can adapt to a new workplace. If the interviewer then said to them, "If you join this company, you'll have to work from dawn to dark. You'll have to give up your dream of becoming a writer. Are you okay with that?" their minds would waver even more. The desire to get a job is strong, but the fear of what they must give up is also significant.

Ambivalence is also common in long-term relationships. People may want to break up because love has faded, yet they want to maintain the stable relationship they've built. Sometimes, even knowing that breaking up would make them happier, they can't overcome the resistance and just complain about their dissatisfaction.

Three Types of Resistance That Hinder Action and Practice

The problem arises when we are unaware of or refuse to accept our resistance. If we are unaware of our internal resistance, we cannot overcome it. Such people try hard but fail repeatedly.

For instance, some avid self-help book readers are overwhelmed by resistance. They try various methods to recover their self-esteem, including reading books, attending lectures, and seeking counseling, but see no progress. Resistance lurks in their minds, sapping their motivation. Reading a book to recover your self-esteem is like reading a manual to become a better driver—it won't help unless you practice driving. Knowledge alone doesn't make one a skilled driver without practice.

If you genuinely want to recover, you must take action. Resistance, however, continually gets in the way. Here are three common types of resistance that keep us from taking the steps to recover self-esteem.

It Won't Work

The first type of resistance is doubt about the outcome. When you start doubting the result, your actions slow down. This doubt arises from a lack of confidence. You think you'll fail anyway, and if you try hard and still fail, it'll feel even more pointless. The thought of hoping for something and not achieving it leads you to believe that giving up in advance might be better.

For someone with low self-esteem, doubting the outcome is natural. They don't trust their abilities, so they can't be sure of success. However, the process of recovering self-esteem isn't about passing or failing. For example, after working out hard at the gym for three months, you may or may not have the perfect body, but you will have definitely made improvements since you started. Even if you only stick to your resolution for three days, it's better than doing nothing at all for three days.

Theory Is Just Theory

When I first read *Men Are from Mars, Women Are from Venus*, I thought that if everyone read this book, there would be no more fights between men and women. It clearly explained the differences in language between men and women and how to communicate accordingly. Although the book became a bestseller, men and women still get into arguments stemming from differences in language.

This is because we have resistance to practice. We separate theory from practice, studying theory diligently but failing to put it into action. If you don't apply what you learn, you will fail, yet some people blame the theory, claiming they failed despite mastering it.

If you have gained insights from reading a book, you need to apply the insights in real life in order to help yourself. Just as theory unrelated to practice is criticized for being abstract, it is not constructive to merely read and not apply what you've learned.

I Tried, but It Didn't Work

Sometimes people try hard but revert to their original state. They may feel their self-esteem improve initially and they may feel more stable, but then everything collapses. They become discouraged by the failure and think, *It really doesn't work.* They feel that all their efforts were in vain.

It takes more than two months to get used to any change, no matter how small. During that time, it's natural for old habits to resurface. Our minds follow the law of inertia.

When this happens, don't blame yourself or give up. Instead, carefully review the reasons and triggers that caused your self-esteem to drop again. Investigate who you met, what was said, and how your emotional response led to this setback. By going through this process, you can put a Band-Aid on the glitch and prevent it from recurring for the same reason.

Keep Going Anyway

You'll encounter many other resistances to change. The influence of people around you cannot be ignored either. They might not recognize your efforts, or while you change, your family might not. A friend might insist you haven't changed even when you have, or you might not feel as happy as you expected. All these things are obstacles you might encounter on the road to change.

Many people wonder how to overcome these road-blocks. The problem arises when people stop the process until they find an answer. In reality, mental barriers are not actual obstacles. They don't literally get in your way, but they tend to make positive results seem less rewarding or make negative consequences feel overwhelming.

If you want to feel real change, it's important to keep going. Sometimes you need to carry on despite not overcoming your mental resistance. As you keep hitting the wall, you'll naturally build strength. Keep putting one foot in front of the other. That brings about change faster.

Believe in the Destination Called Happiness

We all hope to reach the destination of happiness and the recovery of our self-esteem. But fear of the responsibilities or changes that come with these makes us push them away while wanting them. To overcome this fear, you must believe that your destination is waiting for you. Believe that becoming a self-satisfied version of yourself will make you happy. Trust this fact and aspire to it.

Raising self-esteem and becoming happy comes with losses. You must part with the sympathy, care, and concessions you sometimes received when you were unhappy or had low self-esteem. You might receive envy and jealousy along with admiration as you recover. You might suffer from false rumors and unfair situations. It's unavoidable, because while you are changing, others will remain the same, continuing to be immoral and immature.

In the process of recovering self-esteem, you'll undoubtedly face resistance. You might think, *I should have just lived as before,* or worry about no longer being humble. But loving yourself and recovering your self-esteem won't make you suddenly turn into an arrogant person and lead to social ostracism. As you gain self-esteem, you will also develop good manners and consideration for others, which will protect you.

To reiterate, valuing and respecting yourself is the right thing to do. It also makes you happy. We must believe in our happiness. It's certainly nicer to be envied than to be belittled, to evoke jealousy rather than pity. We can be happy and fulfilled on our own without the need for someone's care, and we cannot hurt anyone or cause anyone harm by recovering our self-esteem.

CHAPTER 30

Overcoming Criticism

Criticism is like a virus. It originates from someone's mouth and enters our body. Sometimes this virus spreads within a group, and a trusted friend might even spread it behind your back. That's why we fear criticism and become sensitive to what others say about us.

However, viruses aren't actually that scary. They're not living organisms and lack the physical capability to harm us. The problem arises because they settle in our bodies. Similarly, criticism becomes an issue when we let it get to us. It causes pain and self-reproach within us, attacking us from the inside.

Therefore, it's crucial to recognize when and how criticism is directed at us. Some people are quick to criticize, and it's best to avoid them or keep your distance. If you must be near them, protect yourself as you would against a virus by wearing a mask or washing your hands frequently. In other words, prevent and defend, or at least reduce the aftereffects.

The Five Types of Criticism

First, we need to understand what criticism is, as many people misunderstand it. Is stating a fact or making a well-intentioned comment considered criticism? Not necessarily. Criticism is like shooting an arrow, whether at a friend, at a foe, or at oneself, and it includes the following types:

Cruel Honesty

We learn from a young age to be honest. We are taught that it is commendable to tell the unvarnished truth. What's wrong with pointing out the truth? However, depending on the intention and the accompanying emotions, the act of stating facts can become criticism.

"Parker seems to prioritize family over work."

Suppose Parker hears this from his boss. Even if "prioritizing family over work" is a fact and many people think so, this statement is a form of criticism. The boss's underlying intention is to criticize Parker, and the emotion conveyed is one of dissatisfaction with Parker's focus on family.

Naming Causes

"Is my self-esteem low because I didn't receive enough love as a child?"

This question comes up often in therapy. When mental health issues occur, people often seek its cause. They wonder about the reasons behind their obsession with alcohol, their inability to get over a breakup, or their anxiety.

Therapists must use caution when discussing causes, as it can lead to heated debates among clients and their families. A child might say accusingly, "I'm like this because of Dad!" And a father might defend himself: "It's because you lack willpower! Don't blame others!" These arguments become caught in the pattern of attacking and defending.

Seeking the cause of a negative outcome often leads to criticism because feelings are hurt to begin with. It leads to immature behavior that seeks to assign blame instead of resolving the issue. If finding the cause is essential, do so after considering the other person's feelings and offering sufficient support.

Predicting a Negative Outcome

"If you keep behaving this way, you'll end up a loner. You'll never have any friends."

This is common when raising children or training newcomers. It's meant to caution them with the intention of preventing future mistakes. The downside of this tactic is that it creates a sense of injustice. People who hear this criticism may feel as though they are being accused of stealing a cow when they only took a needle. Repeated and severe criticism can lead to thoughts of *I might as well steal a cow,* turning resentment into rebellion.

Comparing to Others

Most statements that compare are criticisms. For example, a father might say to his son, "So-and-so is such a good son . . ." Trailing off and leaving the rest unsaid is also criticism because the implied message is clear.

While superiors often compare subordinates, subordinates can also compare superiors, expressing dissatisfaction. Children often compare their parents, wishing they were born into wealthier families or had more understanding parents. If kept to oneself, such a statement is less harmful, but once it's said out loud, it becomes criticism.

The Rhetorical Why Question

"Why did you do something you knew you'd regret?" isn't a real question, but instead implies that you are a flawed person who can't correct your mistakes.

Apart from these five types, any comment that makes you feel bad is likely criticism. Even if it seems to be a calm advisory statement or a straightforward stating of cause and effect, if it causes emotional distress, it's criticism because the listener perceives it as such. And it is important to know when you are being criticized.

There's No Such Thing as
Constructive Criticism

When you find yourself being reproached, it's crucial to recognize it quickly. Why? Because criticism doesn't really help us in life. Sure, sometimes a harsh scolding can trigger passion and determination, but that's the effect of ventilation—emotional release through tears—not of the criticism itself.

Some people mistakenly believe that relationships filled with criticism and fighting are somehow developmental. This is particularly common among couples who think that fighting is essential for a healthy relationship. However, most couple therapists strongly disagree. Dr. John Gottman, a renowned American marriage counselor, studied the communication patterns of thousands of couples. He categorized which couples lived happily and which ones were heading toward divorce. His findings revealed that marital satisfaction wasn't rooted in major issues like financial problems, child-rearing, or conflicts with in-laws. Couples headed for divorce had conflicts due to communication styles such as criticism, contempt, and dismissiveness. The main communication style leading to divorce was criticism and retaliation. Phrases like "This is your fault!" and responses like "You're one to talk!" leave emotional scars. Arguing over right and wrong or digging into the root cause of problems in this way brings you one step closer to divorce rather than solving the issue.

Criticism is just projection. It's the act of blaming others when something goes wrong. Projection is an immature defense mechanism. Unlike sublimation or humor, it isn't productive but rather causes more problems.

When a child falls down and bursts into tears, the parent might say, "The ground did it, the ground is bad!" and hit the ground. The child then joins in hitting the ground and stops crying. By blaming the ground, the child momentarily forgets their pain. As the child grows, they learn not to blame the ground because they understand that blaming the ground doesn't heal their scraped knee or turn back time.

However, even adults can lose their sound judgment under stress. When people are distressed to the point of losing their usual composure, even mature individuals revert to using the immature defense mechanisms they used in childhood. The brain temporarily regresses and resorts to criticism.

Frequent criticizing means the mind is often uncomfortable and regressing. Even though nothing is gained and nothing changes, the discomfort in one's mind is so severe that one can't even think rationally.

Things to Remember When Being Criticized

Imagine a boxer in the ring taking punches. If they lose focus, they will keep getting hit until they become befuddled. Even after the match, they will suffer serious aftereffects. Before that happens, they need to duck or clinch. If neither is possible, they should quickly surrender to minimize damage. The same applies when you are being criticized.

Recognize Criticism

Unlike a boxing match, life does not happen in a ring and there's no set opponent. You can be attacked by family, friends, colleagues, or even a passing neighbor. Recognize that you're being criticized and that your defenses are weakening.

Understand That Your Discomfort Stems from Criticism

If you feel bad after meeting someone, it's likely due to criticism. Criticism can come through words, looks, gestures, or even inaction. If it's ambiguous, you've experienced a subtle attack. Asking the person, "Did you just criticize me?" is pointless, as they'll usually deny it. What's important is recognizing that you've been criticized and that you are upset as a result of it.

Acknowledge the Critic's Projections

This point is often overlooked. If someone attacks you, they're projecting onto you because they're troubled. While it's easy to forget this when you're upset, remember that the critic is also distressed. Hurt people say hurtful things.

Realize It's Just Their Emotion

We often believe that critics know us well. If a parent criticizes your personality or a boss belittles you, we accept it as true. However, it's just a fleeting thought from the critic. They aren't authorities on you, have no objective criteria, and no desire or ability to judge wisely. Their opinions aren't truths but personal views that can change anytime. Critics are simply failing to find an effective defense against their own stresses.

How to Handle Question-Form Criticism: Treating Them as Open Questions

Many criticisms come in the form of rhetorical questions. "Why haven't you found a job?" is a criticism in disguise. We need to recognize this.

Instead of retaliating with "Why are you asking me this first thing in the morning?" and inviting further attacks, treat such questions as if the person who asked is actually looking for information. Reflect on why you haven't found a job and respond accordingly: "My language test scores are low." Or "I did not attend a prestigious enough school." If you're unsure, say, "I've thought about it a lot, but I don't know. I'll let you know once I figure it out." Alternatively, ask for their perspective, turning the criticism into a discussion: "I'm not sure why I haven't found a job. Do you have any ideas?"

How to Handle Declarative Criticism:
Simple Acknowledgment of Critic's Opinion

Responding to criticism with more criticism exacerbates conflict. If you retaliate after being criticized, you may get three or four more shots in return. If you take ten shots and give back ten in return, it may balance things out but won't change the fact that you've added to your pain.

Instead, leave your critic's thoughts with them. If your mother compares you to your sister, try responding with "Okay, so what if you think my sister is more intelligent than me?" A follow-up criticism might come, in the form of "Why don't you say you'll try harder like your sister?" Once again, only acknowledge their thoughts: "I suppose that is what you think, Mom."

A Higher-Level Response to
Criticism: Empathy

Critics are often angry, distressed, or hostile toward us. Handling these emotions is challenging. Even therapists face negative emotions from clients all day. We wouldn't last a day on the job if we took it all personally.

Instead, mental health professionals learn to manage criticism by empathizing. Empathy not only heals others but also neutralizes negative emotions effectively. It involves aligning emotional frequencies to erase negative feelings. In conversations, therapists often say, "I see" or "So that's what happened."

Empathy is the most advanced skill for dealing with criticism. For example, respond to a critical boss with, "I'm sorry for delaying and causing you trouble. It must have been frustrating." Empathy disarms criticism, minimizing its impact.

CHAPTER 31

Overcoming Vicious Cycles

When a couple is not getting along, they often believe the problem lies with their partner. They bring their grievances to a therapist, anxious that the therapist might not appreciate how incompetent, mean, or dishonest their partner is. Yet at the same time, they are reliant on their partner. "If only they would change, I wouldn't be so irritable and could be more devoted to our family!" This statement implies their happiness depends on their spouse. Herein lies the irony: They entrust their life to someone they deem the most incompetent person in the world.

Of course they do not easily recognize this paradoxical situation. This issue is not exclusive to couples. Parents who have poor relationships with their children place high expectations on them. Employees who are dissatisfied with their bosses expect a lot from them. The greater the expectation, the greater the disappointment, on top of which the person who let them down is also expected to make up for the disappointment.

Expectation and disappointment create a vicious cycle. The higher the expectation, the greater the disappointment, and the greater the disappointment, the higher the expectation that the disappointing party will make up for it somehow. This cycle repeats until one has to give up, but one usually cannot. When trapped in a vicious cycle, this process continues to reinforce itself. *If I push my husband hard enough, he will change,* a wife thinks, and when he does not change, the disappointment is that much greater.

To Escape This Vicious Cycle, Banish These Thoughts

I need to change the root cause.

Once a mother of two children visited me. She was worried about her two sons. They were two years apart, were very competitive, and often fought over toys. The younger brother would cry when his older brother took his toy. The older brother would then run away, unfazed.

I offered a simple solution: "I think buying two identical toys would solve the problem."

The mother sat there staring blankly for a while. Then she expressed her dissatisfaction in an irritated tone.

"Then the fundamental problem wouldn't be solved."

"Pardon me?"

"We need to solve the fundamental problem. The two boys are too competitive and selfish. I want to raise my children to be considerate and to share. That's why I came here. You need to provide a real solution."

I felt unjustly accused. Her children were only six and four years old. It is completely natural for children to be competitive and try to take things from each other. Moreover, trying to receive more love and attention from their parents is a behavior seen even among adult siblings.

Many people cling to the root cause of problems. It's like standing in front of a fire and pondering, *Why did this fire start? Was it a short circuit? Arson? What are the problems in our country's fire prevention system?* The important thing is to put out the fire first, isn't it?

I need to change other people.

When dealing with mental health issues, people often waste too much energy analyzing the causes, leaving little energy left to solve the problem. A tired brain makes faulty judgments. It obsesses over impossible goals. A typical example is focusing on others. People lose sleep and appetite thinking about others. No matter how much they worry and pay attention, they focus on things they cannot change.

For example, suppose you've been scolded by your boss and then cannot sleep at night. You wake up repeatedly, angry and feeling wronged. The lack of deep sleep leaves you feeling dazed the next day at work. Your concentration drops and your work efficiency decreases. Additionally, your boss is very strict, so you get yet another dressing-down.

The first issue to solve here is to restore your sleep schedule. You need to get a good night's sleep to recover from fatigue. This will improve your work ability again. Most depression can be solved just by sleeping well.

We often forget that other people have problems, too. Your boss has personality issues, and the organizational culture that overburdens lower-ranking employees is also a problem. But if you try to solve those problems first, the symptoms you are experiencing on a personal level will not be resolved. The two things we cannot change in this world are other people and the past. When addressing issues, start with the ones that are within your control.

There is no guarantee that others will change just because you do. Even if you sleep well and improve your work ability, your boss might still find fault in you. But what matters is your life. Others' lives may remain unchanged, but if you change, your own life satisfaction can rise from 20 to 70 percent. Isn't that better?

I need to change my personality.

Some people are obsessed with changing their personality. They seek therapy with a view to fixing their quick temper or introverted nature. Or they claim to exhibit all the symptoms of borderline personality disorder. These people are generally dissatisfied with everything about themselves. But changing one's personality is akin to becoming another person entirely.

Of course, our personalities can change. Some of us change through counseling or sudden epiphanies. The problem lies in calling the problem "personality," which encompasses a great deal. Because the word *personality* generally refers to an inborn trait, we start to wonder if fixing our personality is a viable goal.

Because of this conundrum, people who want to change their personalities get caught in a vicious cycle. For instance:

My personality is awful. I need to change my personality. But personalities don't change easily. Therefore, my personality will remain awful. This is so painful. I need to change my awful personality. But personality doesn't change easily. Medication doesn't help, and neither will seeing a doctor . . . and so on.

If you set about changing your personality as your goal, you will inevitably tire yourself out halfway, putting all your energy into an impossible task. For example, introverts may try to change by attending gatherings and trying to talk more than usual. But every time they feel shy or want to be alone, they are ashamed for feeling this way. And when people don't notice that the introvert is making an effort, as is often the case, the introvert once again confirms, "I haven't changed after all."

In reality, the introvert's efforts will have brought about some changes, but preoccupation with the parts that have not changed will discourage them. It's not that the personality hasn't changed, but rather, obsessing over the parts that aren't changing takes energy and time away from making meaningful changes.

We cannot help but become discouraged when we make changing our personality the goal, because the task itself focuses our attention on the parts of us that we dislike but cannot change.

How to Find and Break the Vicious Cycle

The surface problem and the underlying problem form a vicious cycle. For instance, a deep-seated dissatisfaction with oneself might manifest as dissatisfaction with one's workplace. But dissatisfaction with the external reinforces the deep-seated dissatisfaction with oneself. *I hate this company and I hate myself for working here. I hate myself for letting the company turn me into this person I hate, and I hate the company for making me hate myself . . .* and so on.

Personality issues and relationship problems are similar. The cause is the result, and the result is the cause. When you blame yourself, it leads to blaming others for making you that way, and blaming others leads back to self-blame. Self-reproach and blaming others repeat in an endless cycle.

Repetition generates momentum. When the same phenomenon repeats, it becomes increasingly powerful to the point that the repetition can run on inertia, which then becomes difficult to stop. You need to break this vicious cycle. It doesn't matter whether you break it on the surface or at the heart of the matter; stop blaming yourself or others. Cut it off at the cause or the result.

To break the cycle, you need to understand the cycle you are in. Thinking about it in the abstract may not yield a clear picture, so try writing it down. If you have a self-esteem issue, you've probably thought repeatedly about the causes of your low self-esteem. Now think about the results arising from your low self-esteem and write down the answers to these questions:

What happens as a consequence of my low self-esteem? For example: *I am easily intimidated. I avoid people. I get nervous.*

What happens because of that?
For example: *I can't get a word out on blind dates. I stop seeing people and become lonely.*

What happens because of that?
For example: *I start disliking myself and resent my mother for being overbearing when I was younger. I remember how my ex broke my heart and I start crying.*

What happens because of that?
For example: *I feel pathetic for resenting the past or my family.*

Write it out like this until you circle back to *So my self-esteem gets lower,* which brings us back to the beginning of the vicious cycle flowchart. Then you'll see which step in the cycle is easiest to break. Instead of setting an abstract goal like "raise self-esteem," set specific goals like "don't assign blame" or "forgive the past" to break the vicious cycle. Try making a diagram of the vicious cycle of emotions you feel.

Solve the Immediate Problems First

Doctors use a term called palliative treatment, which means treating symptoms. Even if the underlying cause is easily identifiable, we sometimes need to treat the symptoms or pain first. For example, adolescent acne is caused by rapid physical development and hormonal imbalances. But no doctor stops growth or performs hormone tests to treat acne. The best treatment is to remove the visible acne and prevent secondary infections. Preventing scars and treating visible inflammation while waiting for adolescence to pass is the way to go. By adulthood, the acne usually subsides, so managing it in the meantime is key.

Mental health problems also require palliative treatment. With most issues, it is prudent to put out the fire before examining why one plays with matches around flammable material. Psychiatrists often ask in the first consultation if clients are sleeping well, eating well, and what physical symptoms they are experiencing. They know mental issues are connected to physical problems, particularly basic biorhythms. So they start with symptoms that can be alleviated. They address problems that surface— symptoms that are objectively problematic. These are often physical rather than mental, in the present rather than the past, and about oneself rather than others.

If you've gotten this far in the book and are still suffering due to bad habits or unresolved problems, don't despair. You don't have to eliminate all your flaws to restore your self-esteem. Just acknowledge that you have these traits and keep trying to overcome them.

Low self-esteem is like body fat. While removing unnecessary fat is important, building new muscles is more crucial. Up until now we have focused on eliminating the negative. Now it's time to foster new, positive habits for a healthy self-esteem.

In the next chapter, we will learn practical methods to love ourselves and feel satisfied and secure.

Self-Esteem Class Summary

- If you remove the bad things that harm your mind, recovery becomes easier.
- Everyone has a weak spot in their heart, and it is related to the wounds experienced in the past. Our defense mechanisms are developed from these weak spots.
- Sometimes defense mechanisms that protect the weak spot harm you or others. These are called immature defense mechanisms. The process of healing wounds and recovering self-esteem also includes developing mature defense mechanisms.
- There are two things in this world that cannot be changed: others and the past.
- People want to recover their self-esteem but are often subconsciously resistant to change. We move toward recovery while simultaneously engaging in opposing actions. Understanding and addressing resistance are crucial in the recovery process.
- Three common types of resistance that keep us from taking the steps to recover self-esteem are: "It won't work" (doubt), "Theory is just theory," and "I tried, but it didn't work."
- Criticism, much like a virus, originates from someone's mouth and enters our body. There are five distinct types of criticisms: cruel honesty, naming causes, predicting a negative outcome, comparisons, and rhetorical questions.

- Criticism is just projection. It's the act of blaming others when something goes wrong.
- Empathy not only heals others but also neutralizes negative emotions effectively. This must also be applied to those who criticize us. Empathy disarms criticism, minimizing its impact.
- To escape the vicious cycle of expectation and disappointment, you must banish these thoughts: *I need to change the root cause, I need to change other people,* and *I need to change my personality.*
- Mental health problems require palliative care and treatment.

PART 7

Five Practices to Boost Self-Esteem

CHAPTER 32

Deciding to Love Yourself Unconditionally

We seek love from our parents, expecting them to love us simply because they are our parents. We are taught that parental love is unconditional, that our parents love us just as we are without expecting anything in return. This is what we believe true love to be. When we get married, we also expect unconditional love from our spouses. We say, "This is who I am, love me as I am."

While we desire such love from others, how do we treat ourselves? Rather than loving ourselves unconditionally, we criticize and hate ourselves for a whole host of reasons. The love we should be giving ourselves is the very love we desire from others. We need to love ourselves just as we are, without any reasons or conditions. Our goal is to cultivate an ideal, unconditional love for ourselves.

Love doesn't come because of certain conditions. You don't need to wait until you have an attractive appearance or a good personality. You don't need to wait until you regain self-esteem or become confident. Just decide to love yourself as you are, starting today. Continue to love your personality, your behavior, and even your little habits. That is how you love yourself.

Why We Fear Love

It might seem strange at first to think that deciding to love yourself is the way to self-love. It feels too simple to be true. However, this simple act is so difficult because of our fear of love.

First, there is the fear that loving our weak and insignificant selves will leave us stuck as we are. In other words, we fear that if we love our unappealing appearance and flawed personality, we will never improve or move forward.

Another resistance to love is the fear of narcissism. We worry that loving ourselves too much will make us arrogant. This is like a weak man avoiding exercise because he is worried about becoming too muscular.

Those of us who have long suffered from low self-esteem are skeptical of the power of love. Instead, we believe that loving ourselves will harm us. So we postpone loving ourselves until we become "worthy" of love.

This logic is similar to those who don't give love, saying, "One must be deserving of love to receive love." We treat ourselves this way, criticizing ourselves for not being attractive or confident enough. But what is there to gain from treating ourselves so poorly?

Trust in Love to Love Yourself

Will love really ruin us? Will it cause us to regress or stop us from growing? Will loving ourselves make us arrogant and disliked by others? These conflicting thoughts create an inner struggle. We want to receive love from others, but we feel it's wrong to love ourselves. Sometimes we even reject love from others, fearing that they will leave if they discover who we really are. We do not trust love. We don't trust the words of love or the act of loving others. Fundamentally, we don't trust the power of love itself. We often see love as something negative.

This misunderstanding likely stems from our childhood. We've had many wounds inflicted under the guise of love. We took beatings and insults from those who claimed to love us, who insisted that they did what they did out of love. This has left us confused, misinterpreting love as something that can hurt us.

Love has been misunderstood and falsely accused. Genuine love doesn't destroy anything. Children who are loved and cherished grow up with healthy self-esteem. Narcissism results from a lack of affection. Overprotection stems from the parents' perception that their child is weak. Those who receive unconditional and genuine love grow up to be loving individuals. We need to believe this fact.

It's Okay to Love Yourself

We must now accept that it's okay to love ourselves. There are no good or bad things in love. There is nothing we are or are not allowed to love. Being shy or having low self-esteem does not make us undeserving of love. We should love ourselves as we are right now.

We dream of perfect love, like having someone to stay by your side through recovery from addiction or a terminal illness. Why can't we receive love like that? We often fall into self-pity to see that we are missing this great love in our lives.

We are the ones who should be giving ourselves that perfect love, so let's stop being ambivalent about whether or not to love ourselves.

CHAPTER 33

Loving Yourself

For those who have lived with low self-esteem for a long time, hating or criticizing oneself feels familiar and comfortable. You may feel resistance to learning a new method and tell yourself you'd be better off continuing on as you always have. But we must not give up and must keep learning how to love ourselves. Eventually self-love will naturally permeate your life. There is nothing to lose and everything to gain by loving ourselves.

Find the Loving Person Within

Within each of us, there are three versions of ourselves—the "low self-esteem me"; the "critical me," who disparages us; and the "loving me," who loves us.

The low self-esteem me and the critical me have been battling it out. During the day, the low self-esteem me is active, and at night, the critical me surfaces, attacking everything we did during the day. This causes the low self-esteem me to shrink further, lowering the self-esteem even more.

During this conflict, the loving me has lost its place.

The reason we can't love ourselves is that the loving me has gradually disappeared. It has lost its strength and faded into the subconscious.

Loving ourselves isn't a new thing. It's about bringing the loving me back from the depths of our consciousness. We need to marry the low self-esteem me and the loving me, linking them together. Imagine yourself or a therapist officiating the ceremony, saying, "May the low self-esteem me and the loving me never part and always love each other."

Summoning the Loving Me

The critical me has monopolized our attention, building walls around the low self-esteem me. This blocks messages of love and encouragement from others. But the love from the loving me is still there, strong and consistent. When we hear these messages, we feel happy and grow. We become more loving toward ourselves.

The problem is the defensive wall. The critical me has locked us in, preventing us from receiving these messages. But if we can hear them, the low self-esteem me can grow, become stronger, and even break through the wall.

A mature brain is flexible and able to adapt to different stimuli. For example, if your heart races and you sweat before a presentation, you don't have to get nervous. Let the loving me break through and reassure you: "It's okay! Everyone gets nervous before a presentation. Most of the audience is probably half-asleep anyway. Just read your prepared slides. No one cares if your voice cracks," you can be reassured.

Hearing Messages from the Loving Me

Imagine there is someone who loves you unconditionally. They are completely in love with you. They seem to exist just to love you. It could be a person, a wandering spirit, or even a cat or dog. This being gives you perfect love. What do you think they would say to you? When you are tired, hurting, feeling like nothing is going right, and are disappointed in yourself, what would this person who loves you unconditionally say to you?

When we ponder this question in a relaxed state, we think of answers like: "It's okay. Everyone goes through this." "You did your best. You're amazing just as you are." "I love you. Remember that you are always lovable." These are the words our brains long to hear. Not hearing these words stunts our self-esteem growth. We need to listen to the messages from the loving me. As we hear them, our self-esteem will gradually recover and grow.

To hear these messages, we need to remove the walls built by the critical me. Let's discuss how to break down these rigid walls of low self-esteem.

Breaking Down the Walls
Built by the Critical Me

Our brains consist of many neurons, which form tight loops. Once a thought pattern is established, it tends to repeat itself. The walls built by the critical me are quite real in our brains, reinforcing the negative thought patterns that torment us. It's as if our thought circuits have erected walls.

To break down these walls, we need to stimulate both sides of the brain alternately. Bilateral stimulation, moving left and right alternately, makes brain circuits more flexible.

Walking is a typical bilateral stimulation. As you walk, your left and right brains alternately activate, gradually loosening the defensive walls. Most exercises stimulate the brain, but not all provide bilateral stimulation. Freestyle and backstroke in swimming do, but butterfly and breaststroke do not. Sports like boxing, which use both hands, provide bilateral stimulation, while golf or throwing a ball does not, because they don't engage both sides equally. Eye movement therapy, used for treating PTSD or depression, is an example of bilateral stimulation in therapy. Other methods include touching both sides of the body alternately (like knees or shoulders) and alternating sounds in each ear.

Bilateral stimulation is effective when seeking change. Deciding to quit smoking while walking and repeating "I can quit. I can do this!" is effective. This is why travel is recommended to ease the pain of a breakup.

For boosting self-esteem, I recommend a technique called the butterfly hug, which combines bilateral stimulation with messages from the loving me. Follow these steps:

1. Sit comfortably in a chair with your back supported.
2. Cross your arms across your chest, with your fingers resting on the opposite shoulders or upper arms.

3. Close your eyes and gently tap your upper arms alternately with your palms, one side at a time, at one-to-two-second intervals.

4. While tapping, say to yourself, *It's okay. You did well today. I love you.* Let the loving me speak to you.

This technique can lower the strong defenses built by the critical me and allow messages of love and encouragement to get through, ultimately boosting your self-esteem.

CHAPTER 34

Making Choices and Decisions

People who do not respect themselves often seek others' advice when facing decisions. Some are so overwhelmed by the difficulty of making decisions that they even seek help from mental health professionals. Students contemplating whether to drop out and gain professional experience or to stay in college and prepare for employment, or wives who can't decide whether to divorce their chronically unfaithful husbands, bring their worries to the clinic.

Distrust in One's Judgment

Unfortunately, a psychiatrist cannot make decisions for their clients. The clients know this, of course, but nevertheless pose the question: "You're an expert and have more experience than I do, Doctor. Tell me which decision I won't regret!" Of course, I could answer, "You should not return to school" or "Divorce him. I know a good divorce lawyer." But I deliberately avoid giving direct answers.

Especially with those who are very dependent or express low self-esteem, I approach them with greater caution. I must respect their opinions and help them articulate what they are. They may become impatient, demanding immediate answers. But a psychiatrist who truly respects a client does not make decisions for them. Complying with their wishes in this case would mean disrespecting them.

There Is No Perfect Choice

Life presents us with many crossroads, and we often stand at these intersections, wondering which path to choose—A, B, or C? In most cases, the values of these options are not significantly different, much like deciding between three similar lunch options. Should I have a hamburger, soybean paste stew, or grilled fish? Which choice is the wisest? In reality, the differences are minimal. If we give the hamburger a score of 67, the soybean paste stew might be a 71 and the grilled fish a 69. Over time, these scores can change. The hamburger might initially be a 67, but if there's a special discount at the store, the satisfaction might rise to 72. However, if the discount draws a noisy crowd, the satisfaction could drop to 65.

What's important is that the level of satisfaction is also dependent on who is making the decision. There may be little difference between a hamburger and soybean paste stew, but if your boss takes his employees out to lunch and declares, "Everyone is having soybean paste stew today," the score drops below 50, regardless of how delicious the stew is. Life's major decisions are more serious than lunch menus, but the principle that the level of satisfaction decreases when others decide for us applies. Even if the outcome is good, the joy isn't fully experienced because part of the success belongs to someone else. If the result is bad, it feels even worse.

Less Responsibility for Decisions Made by Others

Decisions come with responsibility. If the decision is entirely yours, you bear 100 percent of the responsibility. But if someone else decides, you bear only 70 to 80 percent at most. Thus, if the outcome is bad, the mental burden is lighter. Regret and guilt are also reduced to 70 to 80 percent. This is why people often avoid trusting their own judgment. In this case, low self-esteem acts as a defense mechanism; avoiding important decisions diminishes our authority but at the same time frees us from responsibility and consequences. If we were to make our own decisions and fail, we would feel 100 percent of the pain and regret, but by having others make decisions for us, we only feel 80 percent of the pain. Consequently, we continue to let others make the same bad decisions because the pain resulting from them isn't so bad.

Decisions Influence Stature

Delaying decisions diminishes our stature in a group. A person with substantial stature makes many decisions, influencing group dynamics and outcomes. A person who lacks decision-making authority has little stature in the group and becomes inconsequential. If we rarely make significant decisions, our self-esteem tends to weaken. This isn't about right or wrong; it's about feeling our own significance in our own lives. To improve our self-esteem, we must train ourselves to make and respect our own decisions.

Self-esteem, on an emotional level, is a feeling of loving oneself. And on a rational level, it is the ability to make and respect one's decisions.

How to Make Decisions to Boost Self-Esteem

Make Decisions Yourself

Make decisions regarding your life. Being the decision-maker in your life brings both power and responsibility, but since your life is your responsibility, this is not a bad deal. When you seek advice, start with "It's ultimately my decision, but I'd like you to weigh in . . ." The key is to decide on your own issues. Focusing on your own choices will reduce unnecessary meddling in other people's affairs.

Act on Your Decisions

Adhere to the decisions you make. When you worry about the road not taken, remember the analogy of the lunch menu. The reason for wavering is that the outcomes are similar regardless of choice. Standing at a crossroads means both options are more or less the same. Don't worry about adverse outcomes; since it's your decision, you will learn a valuable lesson no matter what happens.

Regret with a Future Perspective

Outcomes can be good or bad. If the result is bad, it's okay to feel regret and pain. Take full responsibility and own 100 percent of the pain. However, rather than looking back and beating yourself up over the mistakes you made, look to the future. Try saying, "Next time, I will do this!" This form of regret is a resolution.

Express Gratitude When Outcomes Are Good

Rejoice in good outcomes. Relish 100 percent of the joy. Your decision led to success, and everyone knows your choice was correct. Therefore, share your joy with others: "Thanks to your advice, I succeeded." They will feel good and wish for your continued success.

Five Questions to Aid Decision-Making

There are no right or wrong decisions, nor can we always know which choice is better. What can be clarified in decisions are scope and time. Most decisions pertain to us, thus the scope is limited to you yourself. The remaining factor is time. Be it an hour, two hours, or several years, give yourself a deadline for making the decision. Taking a long time doesn't necessarily yield wiser decisions. It just takes longer.

To respect your decisions, ask yourself:

1. What are the concerns I should be addressing? (Exclude the problems of others.)
2. What needs to be decided? (Exclude emotions.)
3. What are my options? (Place yourself at the crossroads.)
4. When must this decision be made? (Set a time limit.)
5. How long will this decision be valid? (Set the expiration date.)

These questions will help in making decisions. If you continue to ponder beyond the time limit, make that a choice as well. Make the conscious decision to give yourself more time to deliberate, rather than simply missing the deadline and avoiding or delaying a decision.

CHAPTER 35

Focusing on the Here and Now

Plastic surgery ads show before and after photos, making us think about how someone can be transformed. Many ads follow this pattern, focusing on the past and future while skipping over the present. No one makes an ad showing the plastic surgery itself, which would only appear in documentaries.

Desire for change stems from dissatisfaction with the present, so ads skip the present and focus on past and future. However, change in the future is impossible without addressing the present. Plastic surgery entails enduring a great deal of pain in the present. That is the reality.

If you wish to change, you need surgery of the mind. This involves a little pain and patience as well. Yet many avoid this, constantly oscillating between past and future, ignoring the present.

All Solutions Lie in the Present

"Can you change me? If I receive therapy, will I be able to love myself?" I get these questions often via email or phone.

They're tough to answer. When asked about the future, my response is usually the same: "I don't know." People keep asking about what's to come years later when we hardly know what will happen in the next ten seconds.

To alleviate our anxiety about the future, we make plans. We attempt to combat our fears with self-confidence. This is a popular angle in marketing. Affirmations like "I can do it!" suppress anxiety.

If self-confidence, self-hypnosis, or a positive attitude alleviates your anxiety, it's fine to continue. However, I do not recommend such methods. Despite positive attitudes and optimism, crises will repeatedly occur. When efforts go unrewarded, confidence falters, and we begin to wonder why we are losing confidence. We tend to believe that confidence is the path to success. While confidence is better than constant doubt, the future remains uncertain and confidence in the future isn't essential.

Ultimately, all solutions involve focusing on the present. Despite various methods to alleviate anxiety, reality is unavoidable. At the end of the day, students focus on the material they need to cover for the day, and the person who wants to improve their fitness focuses on their day-to-day workouts.

Escaping to the Past

Even after resolving future anxiety, some fail to focus on the present, retreating to the past. Those who find it difficult to accept reality often cling to past issues.

Asking yourself why assigns blame. "Why did I do that?" leads to blaming yourself. "Why did you do that?" results in resentment toward others. These questions fail to provide answers and only irritate old wounds.

An inability to accept reality causes this backward slide. *Why did he cheat? I don't understand. He told me he was going on a business trip.* Unable to accept the betrayal of a beloved person, we retreat to the past, trying to find answers. This refusal to accept reality stems from the discomfort we feel in the present. Pain or fear drives people to the past in order to avoid suffering in the present.

Self-esteem works in similar ways. When we are dissatisfied with our current selves, we escape to the past. We wonder, *Was it a problem from kindergarten? Was it because my parents fought all the time? Or was it the bullying I experienced in high school?* We keep running away like this. But the answer we reach at the end of these questions is always the same: *I feel so pathetic for wasting so much time obsessing over the past.*

Seeking What I Want Here and Now

Obsession with the past leads to regret, while focusing on the future causes confusion. The past is unchangeable, thus frustrating, and the future is unknown, thus anxiety-producing. This is the nature of the past and the future. Healthy individuals balance their focus among past, present, and future, with a bias toward the present. People with low self-esteem tend to be preoccupied with past or future problems.

The solution begins with focusing more on the present. This is the principle psychiatrists call focusing on the here and now. It means not thinking about past problems or future worries but concentrating on what needs to be done at this moment.

Focusing on the here and now means developing a new habit. It's like exercising every morning or sticking to a certain diet. It's the process of breaking away from our routine and adjusting to a new way of living. However, no matter how much we try to focus on the present, it's easy to get off track, because the here and now is an abstract concept. That's why we tend to escape to future anxieties or past regrets.

To avoid this, we need to write down our thoughts. Right now, take out a piece of paper and write: "What do I want right here, right now?" or "What should I be doing right here, right now?" Then try to answer the question. You might not arrive on the answer immediately, but keep coming back to it, even if you get distracted a few times.

For example, consider someone who has an important presentation in a few days and is anxious about not performing well. They can go through this process to find their own answer:

What do I want right here, right now?
To do well in the presentation.

No, the presentation is in the future. What do I want to do right now?

Now is the time to prepare. But will preparing now help me perform well? Won't I be nervous?

No, that's the future. What do I want right here, right now?

Right now, I want to prepare hard, but it's already eleven p.m. I went to see a film with a friend after work. I shouldn't have done that.

That's the past. What do I want right here, right now?

Right here, right now, I want to focus for an hour and organize my presentation materials.

Okay, then let's write that down: "I want to organize my presentation materials for an hour right now."

Stick the note above your desk. Look at it whenever you feel anxious about the future or regretful about the past. This will help you concentrate on organizing your materials.

Focusing on the present not only accelerates problem-solving but also brings new benefits. One of these benefits is charm. People who are immersed in the present appear very attractive. By increasing your self-esteem and focusing on the present, you also gain charm. It's a triple win.

CHAPTER 36

Breaking Through Defeatism and Moving Forward

Even if you tell people trapped in defeatism how to improve their self-esteem, they say they don't know how to do it. They don't know how to love or how to respect their decisions. If you tell them to exercise, they say they can't do it.

There's no point in arguing with these people because of the emotional weight that self-esteem carries. They seem logical, but in fact their emotional self-esteem is low.

However, there is still a way out in this case. Even if you are immersed in defeatism or know nothing about self-esteem, there is a way. It's like learning how to drive a car without knowing how it works. Self-esteem is the same. Even if you don't know what self-esteem is or why it should improve, it can still be improved.

The Weaker the Self-Esteem, the Firmer the Belief

People trapped in defeatism are certain. They are certain that they will not succeed. And they can even provide evidence: "I won't succeed because of this and that. Taking medicine won't help, counseling won't help. Ultimately I have to change, but I can't change." If you think that people with low self-esteem are unsure of themselves and unable to make decisions, you're wrong. They are firm in their beliefs—especiallly in their unshakable belief that they will not succeed. This is because they concentrate on negative evidence. They only recall their weaknesses, wounds, deficiencies, and unsuccessful careers. They reinforce negative conclusions based on negative evidence.

Of course none of us wants to have such a negative view of ourselves. However, it is not easy to change firm beliefs. It's a kind of delusion or faith. It offends us when someone tries to tell us we can change. We cry, "Do you know me? I know best how I've lived. So don't try to convince me otherwise—I can't be happy!" Advice like "love yourself" or "respect yourself" falls on deaf ears. We may cite numerous data and evidence to refute the advice.

From the Ruins to a Comfortable Home

Self-esteem is like a house. No matter how harsh our reality, we can endure it if we have a comfortable home.

Many criticisms attacking the mind and miserable external circumstances are akin to bad weather in this analogy. Self-esteem must be strong to safely find shelter from the elements and calm the mind and body.

People accustomed to defeatism are like people accustomed to living in a house that is badly in need of repair. The house has poor insulation against the cold, and the roof leaks so badly that it is ready to collapse at any moment. The water pressure is very low, and the house has not had a thorough cleaning in a long time. They crouch in one corner of the house, thinking to themselves, *I've lived like this since I was a child. My parents lived like this, too. There are people who live worse than me, so what?* Acquaintances try to help them. People come over to clean and cook for them. But once they leave, the house returns to square one. Even if experts come and repair the house and offer the occupant a temporary shelter in the meantime, the occupant declines because they will have to organize and throw away a few beloved items ahead of the renovation. They don't want change. They prefer what they are used to rather than progress.

But even in such cases, self-esteem can change. It doesn't matter if you're not ready to accept it. I've compared self-esteem to a house, but the process of improving your self-esteem doesn't require construction. When a run-down house is being renovated, the residents must vacate it. You have to demolish the existing structure, which creates noise and dust. However, there is no need for such a cumbersome process when rebuilding your self-esteem.

The Miraculous Question: What If My Self-Esteem Was Restored?

Restoring self-esteem makes the brain healthier. It leads to positive thinking and prevents trivial worries. It is not easily affected by others' emotions and does not lose faith in its own judgment. But the reverse is also true: With a healthy brain comes healthier self-esteem.

There are two things to keep in mind to restore brain health:

First, the brain is a physical organ. Simply thinking about getting a healthy brain is like hoping muscles will appear in your arms just by wishing it. Mind control is also necessary, but you need to lift heavy dumbbells to build actual muscles. Taking action is important.

Second, the distinction between efforts for brain health and its results is not always clear. So if you behave like a person with restored self-esteem, the brain becomes healthier and restores self-esteem.

Imagine that a miracle happened overnight: What if you woke up one morning to find your self-esteem completely restored? Imagine being a warm person who loves and respects yourself. You've become confident and trust your own judgment, and you are considerate of others. When dawn breaks, how would you behave differently from yesterday? Some of my clients answered this question like this: "I think I would smile when I looked in the mirror. It's always painful to look in the mirror every morning. If my self-esteem improves, I won't frown at myself as I wash my face and I might hum while taking a shower." Or: "I think I would finally have breakfast. Before, I would eat late at night, so my stomach would be upset, and I'd wake up after fitful sleep. I didn't feel like eating in the morning and I went to work feeling like I wanted to die. But now I think I'll have breakfast or maybe a simple salad."

Do that behavior first. The brain follows your actions by confusing cause and effect. It gets easier as you go along. You and your brain will adapt.

Three Habits for a Happy Brain

These are simple and effective ways.

Walk the Walk

Walk like a person who respects themselves and trusts their decisions. You will find yourself standing taller, and your shoulders will relax. Walk like someone perfectly at ease, who doesn't care about criticism from others.

Look at Yourself with Love

Whenever you look in the mirror, think about what expression you would wear if you loved yourself right now, and make that face. If you're feeling okay, you'll end up smiling. I won't force you to smile. In life, there are days when you break up with your lover or someone in your family is sick. Even on such days, think about what expression you would be wearing if you loved the person in the mirror. And make that face.

Talk to Yourself

When you're going through a tough time, think about what people with strong self-esteem would say to themselves, and say that to yourself. You might generalize by saying, "It's okay, everyone goes through this," or rationalize by saying, "I have managed this situation well because I'm capable. If it were someone else, it might have led to a bigger accident." Tell your brain that. The brain likes such words. Tell the brain what it likes as often as you can.

Keep in mind walking the walk, looking at yourself in the mirror, and talking to yourself like someone with high self-esteem. These are actions only humans can choose to take. The human brain functions actively when performing these three actions. When the brain is most active and efficient, enhancing self-esteem brings about change. Screaming, breaking things, and attacking others are actions that other animals can also take. With such actions, you cannot restore brain health. Let's live like sophisticated humans.

Self-Esteem Class Summary

- We need to love ourselves just as we are, without any reasons or conditions. We should love ourselves as we are right now.

- Within us, there are three versions of ourselves: the "low self-esteem me"; the "critical me," who disparages us; and the "loving me," who loves us.
- Allowing others to make decisions for you can lead to dissatisfaction, especially if the outcome is negative.
- To improve self-esteem, we must train ourselves to make and respect our own decisions.
- There are four things to remember when making decisions to boost your self-esteem: Make the decisions yourself; act on your decisions; regret with a future perspective; and express gratitude when the outcomes are good.
- Obsession with the past leads to regret, while focusing on the future causes confusion and anxiety. The solution begins with focusing more on the present. All solutions lie in the present.
- Focus on the here and now principle.
- These are three habits for a happy brain: walking the walk, looking at yourself with love, and talking to yourself like someone with high self-esteem would.

EPILOGUE

You Are the King of the Jungle

For a long time, I thought lions were literally the kings of the jungle. I thought they would hunt freely, play with their cubs, and hunt casually if they were hungry. I thought all animals fled when the lions appeared—zebras and gazelles, even elephants or crocodiles.

I only recently learned that a lion's life is not as easy as I thought. I saw a lion being attacked by a hippopotamus on the National Geographic channel. It was the revenge of a hippopotamus mother who had lost her calf. The lion was left barely alive after the hippo attack, writhing on the ground. I was shocked. That wasn't all. The lion's day-to-day life also looked quite difficult. Eagles, hyenas, and other predators threatened the lair whenever possible, and they were anxious about their cubs being attacked. Even hunting alone was not easy. Zebras are surprisingly fast and can kick lions with their hind legs. The kicks are powerful enough to shatter a lion's jaw. The lion sometimes fled in terror, fearing it would be bitten by a snake or trampled by an elephant.

My eyes filled with tears as I watched the weary lion. I had wanted to be like the lions I had envied so much, but a lion's life was a daily struggle as well.

I think that perhaps our lives are similar to that of a lion. Living in contemporary society, we might all be living the life of a sad lion. We want to be at the center of the world, our families depend solely on us, but the world is full of threats. Even though we are already struggling, we must sprint constantly and outrun others just to survive. Like weary lions, we are enduring the jungle that is the world.

But what if we look at it this way: Though we are momentarily exhausted by the demands of parenting and daily life, we are all magnificent and superior to lions. To our families, we are irreplaceable sons, daughters, parents, and spouses. We are warriors who have endured many crises and heroes who have steadfastly protected others. Sometimes we might lose our balance from unexpected attacks and cry out in sorrow and despair, but the fact remains that we are kings. It's okay to cry silently in a dark room. We don't cry because we are weak but because we are human.

Never ever forget that you are the king of the jungle. You are the center of the world. You are a precious being, the only one of your kind in the world.

Index